SEX ADJUSTMENTS
OF YOUNG MEN

SEX ADJUSTMENTS
OF YOUNG MEN

By

LESTER A. KIRKENDALL, Ph.D.

ASSOCIATE PROFESSOR OF EDUCATION
TEACHERS COLLEGE OF CONNECTICUT
NEW BRITAIN, CONN.

Foreword by
PERCIVAL M. SYMONDS

McGrath Publishing Company
College Park, Maryland

1970

Reprinted by
McGrath Publishing Co., 1970

ISBN: 0-8434-0086-2
LC # 77-119237

Reprinted from the copy at the
Library of Case Western Reserve University

Manufactured by Arno Press Inc.,
in the United States of America

TO
C. R. S.

CONTENTS

....

[VII]

FOREWORD

THE CHANGE in attitude toward sex by American society
is one of the striking shifts in sentiment in this generation. It is difficult now to put oneself in the frame of
mind which was universal before the World War. Discussions and conversations about sex were then strictly
taboo. Books could be published only illicitly and then
were not subject to general circulation. Sex was made to
appear as something to be ashamed of, nasty, and repul-
sive. Then the War came and after it a wave of exciting
freedom and license. The fight against a prudish attitude
toward sex was not without resistance. But the relaxa-
tion of the attitude of the courts toward the publication
and general circulation of books dealing seriously and
scientifically with matters of sex reflect the change. In
no way was this more clearly exhibited than by the decision to publish for general distribution Havelock Ellis'
Studies on the Psychology of Sex.

Dr. Kirkendall's book is directly in line with the current trend. He is writing to young men about the sex
problems of young men. He writes from his own first
hand evidence gathered from talking with scores of
young men about their sex problems. Many of those
with whom he talked were able to discuss their problems
with him only with the greatest difficulty because of the
secrecy and sense of shame with which they surrounded

their difficulties in phantasy. Any young man who reads the experiences related by the cases included in this book will recognize that his experiences and his feelings are not unique with himself. And by virtue of this he may be relieved of a feeling of his own inadequacy or guilt and thereby be encouraged to face his own problems more openly and intelligently. This book, then, should have a very healthy influence in helping young men to face sex in their own lives without the hush that so commonly surrounds it.

I can recommend Dr. Kirkendall's book to young men as a scientifically sound yet simple discussion of the problems of sex.

PERCIVAL M. SYMONDS

Teachers College, Columbia University
New York

[x]

PREFACE

THIS VOLUME is the culmination of twelve years of counseling work with boys and young men. During friendly conversations with them in regard to various matters of personal adjustment, questions often arose relating to maturing sex urges, habits, and desires. With increasing contacts and widening knowledge, I came to believe that I was securing information regarding the sex adjustments of youth different from that commonly found in writings on the subject. The young men so frequently expressed the belief that the attitude taken and the information given was helpful, that I was encouraged to extend my inquiries to find, insofar as possible, the facts concerning common adjustments within the age period of sixteen to twenty-five. Using the information thus obtained as a basis, I have put into written form the suggestions usually made in counseling, hoping they may prove helpful to other young men, to counselors, and to parents.

Much of the material usually contained in a preface I have chosen to put in Chapter I. I feel that to get an adequate understanding of sexual adjustments, it is necessary for the reader to have not only accurate information, but a considered attitude as well. Therefore, the first portion of the book has been devoted to an attempt to assist in the building of desirable attitudes toward sex.

[XI]

Discussions of the physical structure of the sex organs are omitted. It is taken for granted that the reader is sufficiently familiar with the anatomy of the human body to make these unnecessary, but for those who wish further information concerning anatomical structure there are several references in the bibliography at the end of the book.

I acknowledge with appreciation permission from the following publishers to quote from their books: Association Press; McGraw-Hill Book Company, Inc.; Albert & Charles Boni, Inc.; D. C. Heath and Company; Reynal and Hitchcock, Inc.; D. Appleton-Century Company; and Random House, Inc. Dr. Eric M. Matsner of the American Birth Control League has kindly extended permission to quote from his pamphlet, "The Technique of Contraception," and has offered helpful and authoritative suggestions on several points. Mr. Kenneth Peterson, instructor in Greeley (Colorado) high school has extended permission to quote from his thesis, "Early Sex Information and Its Influence Upon Later Sex Concepts."

While I alone am responsible for the contents of this book I should like to express my appreciation for the counsel and help of various persons. Dr. R. G. Gustavson, Chairman, Department of Chemistry, University of Colorado; Dr. Maurice A. Bigelow, Educational Consultant of the American Social Hygiene Association, and Professor Emeritus, Teachers College, Columbia University; Dr. Paul Popenoe, Director of the Institute of Family Relations, Los Angeles; Dr. Lewis M. Terman, Stanford University, Palo Alto, California; and Dr.

Robert L. Dickinson of New York City, have given suggestions on specific points.

A number of persons have read the manuscript and made valuable suggestions. Grateful acknowledgment is made these, particularly to Dr. Richard L. Wampler, Teachers College of Connecticut; Dr. Frank C. Jean and Mr. Darrell Barnard, Colorado State College of Education; Mrs. Sidonie M. Gruenberg of the Child Study Association, New York City; Dr. Mehdi Nakosteen, Denver, Colorado, and Dr. Paul Popenoe. Dr. Percival M. Symonds, Teachers College, Columbia University, was especially helpful.

To Mr. Fredrick McKone, Meriden, Connecticut, I am indebted for the suggestion that in referring to the other sex the word "other" be used as expressing a complementary relationship, rather than the word "opposite" which implies a contrariety or opposition in relationship.

To Mr. Charles Shaw, New Haven, Connecticut, especial thanks are due for untiring work on the manuscript, for discerning criticism, and constant interest and helpful suggestions.

To the young men who have given me information which makes it possible for me to understand their problems more thoroughly, I extend thanks. I hope their frankness will make it easier for others to reach an adequate understanding of the part sex can play in building a wholesome individual and social adjustment.

LESTER A. KIRKENDALL

SEX ADJUSTMENTS
OF YOUNG MEN

Chapter I

SOCIAL AND INDIVIDUAL ATTITUDES TOWARD SEX

WE LIVE in a society which, in the past, has been unwilling to speak straightforwardly about sex. For the most part this unwillingness still exists. Parents and their maturing children usually find it impossible to discuss the subject openly, even when the occasion makes it important to do so. Often this is because of a lack of intelligent understanding based upon accurate knowledge. It is the purpose of this book to supply such knowledge and understanding. It is intended for young men who have reached the age of sex maturity, and who wish to determine the most satisfactory sexual adjustment before marriage.

This discussion will be of maximum help if you approach it seeking a solution to the questions concerning sex adjustment. Too often books of this kind are read to secure a vicarious or second-hand sex satisfaction. The reader skims through the book selecting the sensational features, and perusing the description of individual cases, but omitting the rest of the discussion. Possibly he will inject his own thoughts, which may be lewd or inaccurate, into the discussions of the author. As a result he finishes reading the book as poorly prepared

[1]

to meet the issues of sex adjustment as he was before he began. For example, while this book was in manuscript form it was handed to two professional men, well past middle age, who had expressed an interest in what had been written. The manuscript was returned with underlinings and bawdy marginal comments. Obviously their adjustment to sex was so poor that they could not read the manuscript without transferring to it their own sexual inadequacies and misconceptions. You will receive the greatest benefit from reading this book if you can free yourself of erroneous attitudes and accept readily the points of view suggested in this chapter. Do not read to secure a vicarious form of sex stimulation. To be seriously interested in the facts relating to adjustment and in the issues involved is highly desirable; to seek suggestions in your reading for rationalizing a course of action is not.

SOURCES OF INFORMATION

The information upon which this book is based comes from several sources. First, from hundreds of conversations with young men during which questions relating to their individual sex adjustments were discussed. The discussions were organized so that certain points were raised in each interview. The information relating to these points was recorded and later organized to show the extent to which the various adjustments were used. In a number of cases it has been possible, through the cooperation of individual young men, to study their sexual adjustments over a period of several years to observe their persistence or change. This has been particularly helpful in gaining a fuller understanding of the various methods followed in adjusting to sex. All persons whose sexual adjustments have been described have been personal acquaintances of the author. The information relating to each has been used by permission, and has been checked carefully for accuracy.

Since most of the individuals have been college or university students, the discussions may give a somewhat atypical picture of male adjustments. These young men are undoubtedly above the average in intellectual ability, but it is an open question as to whether they have had a moral education better than that of the average home. If there is a bias as a result of selection, it is probably toward more socially acceptable adjustments than would be found in similar age groups of casually chosen young men.

A previous study by Hughes* affords some reason for expecting such a bias. After collecting and studying information concerning sex experiences and practices from high school boys, mill boys, and preparatory school boys he wrote: "Figures obtained from the last three questions [on masturbation] indicate that there was more indulgence among mill boys than among school boys, and that the frequency of masturbation was highest and the length of time the practice was continued was longest among mill boys. [But] these comparisons should be viewed with caution."

In reading the cases cited in this book one is likely to be impressed with the seriousness and objectivity with

* Hughes, Walter L. "Sex Experiences of Boyhood." *Journal of Social Hygiene.* 12:262-273, May, 1926.

which these young men considered sex, but it would be a mistake to infer that all young men, or indeed, all of those with whom I have talked, regard sex in this manner. Some are interested in it chiefly as a source of pleasure; sex to them is a plaything, a means of personal physical satisfaction. I have not included a large number of cases illustrating this particular phase of adjustment, but it is important to recognize its existence.

The cases included are not necessarily typical nor are all of them intended to indicate best practices. They are used in the discussion for the purpose of describing situations. For the most part, however, they concern individuals who, on the whole, were making excellent social and personal adjustments. Men who are mentioned have been academic leaders of their classes in school, honor students, class presidents, members and officers of fraternal and social groups, leaders in church and community affairs and interested in cultural activities. At the beginning of each case descriptive terms are used to permit the reader to judge for himself the general social and scholastic standards attained by the individual whose sex adjustments are under consideration. Emphasis is given this point to show that the necessity for making such adjustments is not peculiar to a certain group. It transcends lines of class and economic status.

Every young man, regardless of his social station and intellectual ability, is aware of certain desires and interests arising with sex maturity. The fact that young men holding positions of social and scholastic leadership in the community have difficult problems of sex adjustment is no indication of abnormality. Any normal youth

[4]

may meet difficulties as he attempts to adjust to a maturing physiological drive having psychological and social implications. The knowledge that he is by no means atypical if he meets such difficulties should encourage him to face his problems of adjustment squarely, frankly and objectively.

As a second source of information, a study of the best literature available has been made to compare the conclusions reached in this book with those of authorities in the field, particularly with respect to such phases of sexual adjustment as seem to arise in the experience of the average boy. The more marked abnormalities of sex adjustment have been regarded as outside the scope of this discussion.

Third, I have studied literature pertaining to sexual adjustments found in other societies, particularly in earlier civilizations, to gain a better understanding of the problems commonly found in our monogamous society where biological maturity is reached, in most cases, a number of years before marriage occurs.

Fourth, my own personal experiences and those of my friends as we were growing from boyhood into youth and manhood have given me a first-hand realization of the problems which arise at the time of maturity, and a keen awareness of the need and desire for accurate and authentic information on the part of youth.

ATTITUDES ADVERSELY INFLUENCING SEX ADJUSTMENTS

If a satisfactory adjustment to the sex urge is to be made, correct attitudes with respect to sex must be formed. My experience in talking to young men has

[5]

convinced me that before information can be given and acted upon intelligently, certain definite attitudes are essential. Frequently this means breaking down previously formed concepts which interfere with alterations of adjustments or even make them impossible. The first problem then for a young man desiring to think intelligently about his adjustments to sex, is to examine his points of view toward sex. This is the first problem in our discussion.

Whether one adjusts to sexual urges easily and wisely, or so poorly that his future happiness is jeopardized, depends largely upon how he looks at sex. If he can form an attitude enabling him to evaluate it calmly and objectively in relation to other phases of living, he will have taken an important step toward good adjustment, but if his attitudes are conflicting, prudish, or lustful, it is important for him to recognize it. The reason for this will become increasingly evident in the following discussion.

Attitudes are not altered by a mere decision to vary them; if changes are desired, clear thinking based upon accurate, scientific information, and free, objective discussions is necessary to produce them. Unfortunately it is often difficult to obtain adequate information from competent sources. The instruction in sex which young men receive is all too often such as to produce a distorted concept of the whole matter. This "misinformation" passed along from person to person, in out-of-way places, the pool-room, the back-alley, or in secret "bull sessions," almost always creates erroneous impressions. For example, the young men who have no other source of knowledge may come to believe that sex is mysterious and secretive, that nice people never mention it, or that its single function is to provide physical gratification. These concepts are so deeply rooted that they are exceedingly difficult to change but they play an important part in building individual attitudes.

Before right attitudes can be created, it is necessary to be able to recognize those based upon misconceptions for what they are. One of the common attitudes which block clear and intelligent thinking is that which regards sex as shocking, disgusting, and ugly, to be mentioned only when it is unavoidable. Silence is preferred, and maintained if at all possible. A discussion of sex with persons holding this attitude is out of the question. Their embarrassed, uneasy, and confused manner is communicated to others. Often parents are unable to approach a discussion of sex in an objective and reassuring way. They may not regard it as shocking or ugly, but their embarrassment and confusion create the impression in their children that sex is something about which it is undesirable or impossible to speak freely.

One adolescent boy, for example, found a book on sex on his dresser one day. While nothing was ever said he was certain it came from his parents. Their reluctance, or inability, to discuss openly such matters as physiological sex maturity, or relationships between the sexes produced a similarly evasive treatment on the boy's part, at least as far as willingness to talk with his parents was concerned. In another instance a father handed his son a good scientific treatise on sex. He hesitated, and then, in an embarrassed manner said to the boy, "Here, read

[7]

this, and come back to me if you have any questions." Both boys may have secured the essential physiological facts about sex. But there is no doubt that each gained the impression that sex was a topic to be avoided; and, after these awkward approaches, free discussion with their parents was impossible. Actually it is this attitude which does much to produce the feeling that sex is unwholesome. Suppression and furtive treatment give an atmosphere of mystery and impurity which results in distorted behavior.

A second common attitude which stands in the way of careful thinking prohibits a complete and detailed discussion of sex adjustments. Many times adults who counsel with young people do not realize the importance of giving them a body of information which they can use in drawing their own conclusions. Parents, teachers, and others often feel that fragmentary and haphazard information is all that is necessary or desirable. Often parents seem to feel that if they warn their children against social diseases or sexual relationships they have given enough attention to the matter. Possibly their own background has been so limited that they can do nothing else. A major difficulty in sex education is that few parents or teachers know enough to be able to give detailed and adequate suggestions.

The inquiries of most young men touch upon so many phases of sex that a thorough explanation of specific points is needed. Many discussions consist only of veiled warnings, vague references, and indefinite suggestions. For desirable sexual adjustments a wide range of knowledge is essential. More harm will arise from knowing too little than from knowing too much.

Another attitude often found among people who have had lustful associations with sex is that it is to be indulged in only for personal pleasure and sensual satisfaction. Young men with this viewpoint come to have little or no care for the social consequences of their behavior. They think solely of physical satisfaction and take considerable pride in the rapidity and number of their conquests.

For individuals to wish to experience the physical pleasures of sex is perfectly normal and desirable. Such satisfactions are an integral part of a satisfactory sexual life. It is when they become an end in themselves that danger enters. Sex then is isolated from its social relationships, and the enjoyment of physical pleasure becomes a search for the sensual. Sexual experiences, entered into with due regard for the personal adjustments of others and for the social consequences, are among the most satisfying and enriching of all experiences. But the young man or woman who looks upon the sex act as simply a physical act is in a fair way to deprive himself or herself of the richer experiences that come when sex is regarded as a positive, constructive force in living.

A fourth undesirable attitude is quite the opposite of embarrassment, confusion, and vagueness. Revolting against inhibitions and prudishness, the persons holding this attitude disregard all restraint, and exhibit instead a pronounced immoderateness in discussions concerning sexual conduct and behavior. This attitude is as extreme and as undesirable as the first two mentioned. That prud-

[9]

ishness and undue reticence should be broken down no careful student of sex denies; yet the desirable alternative is not absence of all restraint, with sex a constant topic to be shouted from the housetops.

We speak freely of our physical disabilities or intellectual uncertainties when open discussion of them will assist in their solution, but we do not keep them always on parade. The same should be true of sex. The constant flaunting of the subject with flagrant disregard for all conventions relating to it indicates a maladjustment as clearly as does a marked reluctance to speak of it. There is a tendency to swing from the extremely prudish to the extremely blasé. Both are socially undesirable. The most desirable attitude, which is found between these two extremes, eliminates the lewdness from sex, regards it as a constructive factor in living, and permits objectivity and directness in the consideration of matters of adjustment.

ATTITUDES ADVANTAGEOUSLY INFLUENCING SEX ADJUSTMENTS

Throughout this book references will be made to desirable social attitudes toward sex. Consequently, an elaborate discussion will not be given here. There are, however, several important attitudes which will help in building intelligent sex behavior that should be briefly mentioned. These are basic to the succeeding chapters, and should be kept in mind while reading.

In the first place, it is essential to realize that the question of what sex adjustments shall be used must be answered by everyone. To know this dispels the feeling of being the only one who has ever had to face such problems. Struggling in solitude is apt to lead one to believe that his situation is unique. The truth is that at one time or another practically every boy experiences a feeling of being different and alone. This is especially true of those who practice masturbation,* though this feeling may arise from struggling with sexual urges, mental preoccupation with sexual matters, frequent erections, unexplained seminal emissions, homosexual drives, feelings of guilt with regard to sexual desires, or other unexpected and disturbing manifestations of sex.

As one comes to know more about the patterns of sexual conduct followed by young men these patterns come to assume a marked similarity. As a young man learns more about the manifestations of sex and its psychology, he finds that his questions and problems are very similar to those of other persons of his age. In the second place, an attitude permitting an open and unemotional consideration of sex needs to be developed. If one is to achieve a good adjustment he must be able to speak as directly and freely of sexual matters as of habits of proper diet or sleep. Correct habits of sex behavior can be learned in the same way correct habits can be learned in any other field. Rather than feeling ashamed of a desire to know the answers to questions relating to sex, one should feel ashamed of an unwillingness to face the questions. The wish to discuss sex problems is perfectly

* Masturbation refers to stimulation of one's own sexual organs to obtain sexual satisfaction. Usually it involves the production of an orgasm, or climax, at which time a discharge of semen, the reproductive fluid, occurs. Masturbation is usually brought about by the use of the hand, but there are other ways in which it can be produced.

[11]

normal and, if the discussion is for the purpose of achieving a more satisfactory adaptation to the drive, it is desirable.

Many a young man has found that a frank discussion of sex with someone who could discuss it objectively resulted in an attitude which was in a greater degree freed of bias and prejudice, and which in turn decreased or eliminated his worries and difficulties. If embarrassment and hesitancy are felt in confidential discussions with a person who is informed and direct in his approach, it implies the need for a more objective adjustment. One should also respect other young men who show an objective interest in straightforward discussions of sex, whether that interest arises from an actual need for assistance, or from a simple desire for further information. A prevalent attitude among young men is that if any one of their number asks openly for information about problems of sex he must be poorly adjusted. This often makes discussion difficult and hampers the alteration of biased and illiberal attitudes. A genuine interest in the best personal adjustment should be regarded as indicative of good rather than poor adjustment.

In the third place, an attitude which emphasizes a proper respect for social conventions is important in serving as a check upon hasty and ill-considered behavior. All social conventions may not be correct, but many undesirable consequences may grow out of violating them, particularly in matters of sex. Social conventions with respect to sex are changing, of this there can be no doubt. But flagrant violations, with utter disregard for those with whom we do not agree, are not advisable. Individual changes should be made only after due consideration of all factors involved. A more detailed discussion of this point as related to the problem of sexual intercourse before marriage will be found in Chapter IV.

In the fourth place, the attitude that sex is a universal force which can make genuine and permanently satisfying contributions toward a well-balanced life should be of marked help to those individuals who feel that all sexual satisfactions in some way smack of evil. Rightly conceived, sex is not to be used solely for sensual pleasure, nor is it a force which must always be watched carefully and controlled meticulously lest it cause trouble. Though sex is sometimes spoken of in this book as a problem, it is not one which will necessarily cause distress. Sex, in and of itself, does not create difficulties for us—rather the difficulties, when they do occur, grow out of our lack of understanding of the place of sex. The proper ordering of the sex life is an important factor in the establishment and maintainence of a happy family life, and for most young men this aspect of living sooner or later assumes an important place. Marriage and family rearing are phases of activity which most people carefully plan for and cherish. If the possibility which sex offers for a great and positive contribution to these plans could be clearly seen, and if, on the other hand, the sorrow and misery which sometimes grow out of an improper use of it could be understood, it is likely that young people would consider much more carefully the sex adjustments they adopt.

One of the best and most certain ways of obtaining a

rational outlook upon sex, to develop a feeling of composure in regard to it, and to learn how to meet the issues of living, insofar as they relate to sex, with satisfaction to yourself and to others for whom you care is to see clearly that sex has possibilities for enriching living, for individual expression, and for providing satisfactions in family life. If the truth could be known probably we would find that worries, uncertainties, and misuses of sex in most cases are associated with a point of view which places sex in a much narrower and less constructive role than is indicated in this paragraph.

In the fifth place, an attitude helpful in achieving objectivity disapproves of lewdness and obscenity at all age levels. The cheap sex joke and the obscene remark indicate an inadequacy in the individual's adjustment to sex. The implication that sex has no humorous associations should not be drawn, but the jokes and remarks to which reference is made here are those which play upon the passions and the mysteries which usually surround sex. They depend for their appeal upon a stimulation of the sexual desires and the achievement of vicarious sexual satisfaction. Talking freely about sex does not necessarily mean that a correct attitude has been achieved. Vulgarity is too often confused with freedom.

A young man who finds that he enjoys cheap sex stories and literature should not be criticized but helped in securing accurate information. Once this is possible, the desire for obscene literature and jokes is likely to disappear. This may not hold true if the attitude of vulgarity has become too strongly implanted. Wholesome attitudes are not built automatically as one grows older. A man of fifty, by risqué conversation and reading, may display an attitude formed during adolescence, which still persists and marks him clearly as being as immature and poorly informed as the most callow youth, even if it does not indicate a more fundamental and deep-seated maladjustment.

A scientific vocabulary is essential in the development of proper attitudes. One must not use "back-alley" terminology with its lascivious and vulgar sexual implications if one is to build proper attitudes. Sometimes parents, in giving information to children, resort to such language, thus creating a feeling of embarrassment on the part of both parent and child which makes it impossible to talk freely. Because these terms have been used by the street-corner gangs in telling obscene stories, or in hinting darkly at the mysteries of sex they have come to be associated with a certain vulgarity which makes impossible their use in any scientific discussion. Discussions of sex are much easier and far more natural if a scientific vocabulary is used. The common vulgar terms with their undesirable connotations should be employed only when they are absolutely necessary to make clear the meaning of scientific terms. To assist in the development of a scientific vocabulary a number of the terms which are most commonly used are included in a glossary found at the end of this book.

Other attitudes might be discussed. Those mentioned here by no means exhaust the subject, but they are the most important ones, and are basic to the ideas advanced in the following chapters.

[15]

In summary, it may be noted that the attitudes discussed in this chapter are classified in two groups. First, there are those which interfere with the building of desirable sex adjustments. These hold that:

(1) Sex is shocking, disgusting, and ugly.
(2) A complete and detailed discussion of sex adjustments should be avoided.
(3) Sex is to be indulged in solely for personal pleasure and sensual satisfaction.
(4) A blasé, flaunting display of sex sophistication should be substituted for all conventions in regard to sex.

The second group includes positive attitudes which assist in creating an intelligent, constructive sex adjustment. These hold that:

(1) Questions relating to sex adjustments are universally a part of normal human development.
(2) Sex may be considered objectively and freed from disturbing emotional associations.
(3) Social conventions in regard to sex should be given thoughtful consideration.
(4) Sex can make a real and positive contribution toward a well-balanced life.
(5) Obscenity and lewdness should always be strongly disapproved.

Chapter II

SEX MATURITY AND ADOLESCENCE

BEFORE BEGINNING a detailed account of specific sex adjustments, we shall consider some of the physical characteristics relating to normal sexual development. This will afford us an opportunity to acquire a better vocabulary, and to understand better some of the physical characteristics basic to sexual adjustments. Since the discussion must be short the explanations will be simplified and phrased in general terms.

By maturity is meant the physical changes which occur at puberty, the time at which a boy or girl becomes sexually capable of reproducing or becoming a parent. It is a gradual process and one cannot specify the hour or day when it is reached; its completion can be judged only by certain physical manifestations.

Evidence collected by physiologists and psychologists indicates a wide range in the ages at which boys and girls reach maturity. If the course of development has been normal, girls reach it at a somewhat earlier age than boys, though the difference is now thought to be less than formerly. The average age of maturity, according to figures collected in the United States, is about thirteen years, six months for girls, and about thirteen and a half to fourteen years for boys.*

* Baldwin, Bird T. *The Physical Growth of Children from Birth to*

[17]

But with both boys and girls there are wide individual variations. In the male, maturity occurs in some cases as early as eleven, and sometimes not until the age of seventeen or eighteen. Failure to mature within these ranges may indicate an abnormality, though psychologists are careful to point out that considerable deviation above or below the average may occur, and yet be regarded as normal. Various factors, such as race, intellectual capacity, health, heredity, nutrition, rest, overwork, and exercise are related to the time of physical maturation.*

The first menstrual flow is commonly considered evidence of sexual maturity in girls. The period of menstruation usually occurs about every twenty-eight days, though there may be a variation of a few days in the cycle of individual women. Also the cycle of any particular individual may vary, so that it is not always regular. The menstrual flow lasts from four to six days. For some women it is a period of acute discomfort, pain, and psychological stress. For others it passes with little or no discomfort. Here again there are individual variations. Depending upon circumstances and general physical conditions, the menstrual period will pass with much less physical discomfort at some times than at others.

The evidences of sexual maturity are more difficult to distinguish in boys. The best single indication is the

Maturity. Iowa City: University of Iowa Studies in Child Welfare. Vol. 1, No. 1, 1921.

Atkinson, R. K. "A Study of the Athletic Ability of High School Girls." *American Physical Education Review*. 30:389-99. 1925.

* Brooks, Fowler D. *Psychology of Adolescence*. Boston: Houghton Mifflin Co. 1929. Page 44.

production of semen, a viscid white fluid generated by the male sex organs for reproductive purposes. Upon maturity semen is given off during sleep, if the individual does not use masturbation or participate in sexual relationships and thus produce an emission. Sometimes these involuntary seminal emissions are delayed past the actual time of sexual maturity. Another evidence of sexual maturity, or approaching maturity, in boys is the growth of hair in the armpits, the appearance of pubic hair around the penis and testicles,* and the increasing size of the sex organs. About this time the voice changes and a growth of downy hair appears on the face. These two last named evidences can be regarded as only approximate indications of maturity.

Since maturity involves physiological changes which in turn influence points of view, one must normally expect to have to make adjustments to this new development. Every young man after the age of puberty will occasionally feel physical drives which are clearly of a sexual nature. These may involve nothing more than occasional erections.† They may result in a sense of

---

* These terms are the scientific words used in referring to the male sex organs. In the mature male, the penis when erect is usually from six to six and a half inches in length and four to four and a half inches around. The testicles, or testes, are the two glands suspended in the pouch of skin just below the penis, called the scrotum. They are oblong in shape and about the size of marbles, or bird's eggs. The testes are sometimes referred to as the gonadal glands.

† An erection refers to a hardening and enlargement of the penis, the male sex organ. In an erection, blood enters the tissues of the penis causing it to grow in size and become unyielding. Erections sometimes occur when the individual is conscious of no conditions of sexual stimulation.

abdominal discomfort caused by an accumulating secretion of semen, or by marked desires for actual sexual contacts. The expression of sexuality is not always the same with every young man nor felt in the same degree, but that there will be some expression seems inevitable.

Since most boys are aware of the changes which are about to take place, maturity is not a surprise to them, but simply an evidence of the approach of manhood. Sex potency is often a source of pride to boys who have just reached puberty, and exhibitions which are intended to prove maturity frequently occur when younger boys come together under circumstances favorable for such exhibitions. Conversations about various phases of sex often take place. Many times younger boys pass along information which they have received from older ones. Investigations have shown that these conversations usually succeed only in spreading inaccuracies and misconceptions. At the same time the use of a lewd, slang vocabulary builds up concepts of sex which must later be broken down if satisfactory adjustment is to be made.

An introduction to various aspects of sex may come at an early age. Many persons assume that a comprehensive awareness of sex does not arise until after physical maturity, but the truth is that few individuals escape some contacts with it before adolescence. Some have casual contacts which leave little impression. On the other hand, these very early contacts may be so vivid that the individual's attitude toward sex is firmly set and therefore very difficult to change.

For example, Exner* found that nearly all children at an early age receive information which determines their behavior and attitudes toward sex. According to his study the average age at which first permanent impressions of sex were registered was nine and a half years. A later study by Hughes† found that the average age at which boys became conscious of sex in such a way that it was a subject for thought and occasional conversation was twelve and a half years. Hughes felt that the difference in average age between the boys participating in his study and those in Exner's was probably due to a difference in the form of question asked.

Peterson‡ asked a group of 419 college men, "How old were you when you received your first information on sex?" and found that sixty-five per cent had received it by ten years of age, and eighty-six per cent by the time they were fourteen.

Problems of adjustment in later life often can be better understood if they are interpreted in terms of early experiences. Premature introductions to sex may come from chance contacts with unfavorable environment or undesirable associates. The studies cited above are unanimous in showing that three-fourths or more of all boys receive their early sex information from such sources as "the talk of other boys," "bull sessions with the gang,"

* Exner, Max J. *Problems and Principles of Sex Education.* New York: The International Committee of Young Men's Christian Associations, 1915.

† Hughes, Walter L. "Sex Experiences of Boyhood." *Journal of Social Hygiene.* 12:262-73. May, 1926.

‡ Peterson, Kenneth M. *Early Sex Information and Its Influence on Later Sex Concepts.* Boulder: University of Colorado. Unpublished Master's thesis. 1938.

or "talks about girls." Marked inhibitions interfering with an open, objective approach to sex or unusual difficulty in achieving proper control of sex desires are examples of the problems which may arise when sex knowledge is gathered from such sources.

The three cases which follow indicate that an acquaintance with sexual practices sometimes comes several years before maturity and produces troublesome problems of sex adjustment for the individual as he grows older.

Gordon—Age 25. High school graduate. Much interested in music and aesthetic pursuits. Associated with a small group of friends with whom he got along very well. Intellectual ability average.*

Gordon was taught masturbation at age six by an older playmate. Later he became worried about the physical ill effects which he thought would arise from the habit, which he practiced five or six times a week. This worry continued throughout adolescence and caused considerable mental disturbance. He tried to break away from masturbation but never succeeded in dropping it for more than a few days at a time. Finally, he reconciled himself to the practice. The frequency with which he resorted to it was lowered, but at age twenty-five it still continued.

Morris—Age 25. University graduate. Gained high honors in scholarship. Personal appearance, handsome. Influential in fraternity life. Wide circle of associates of both sexes.

* As previously stated, the descriptive items used in each case study are included so that the reader can judge for himself the general social and scholastic adjustment of the individuals whose cases are cited.

Morris was introduced to two different sexual practices several years before maturity. At age eight he learned masturbation from watching an older boy. He began the habit at this time and followed it continuously. Between the ages of nine and eleven, before maturity, he was urged to, and attempted intercourse. These early experiences created desires which he satisfied between the ages of fifteen and sixteen by taking up coitus (sexual intercourse) as a habitual form of sexual adjustment. At age twenty-five he estimated that he had had sex relations with twenty-five or thirty girls. Masturbation was continuous from eight to fifteen, and has continued from fifteen until the present, except when intercourse has been used in its stead.

Olen—Age 22. College junior. Honor student. Well liked by associates. Quiet and reserved. Universally respected for his high character.

When about seven, an incident of homosexuality occurred in the neighborhood of Olen's home and Olen was sternly warned by his parents to have no sexual associations, nor to talk to anyone about sex. A short time later he entered a public toilet, and observed a man who was, he thought, looking at his (Olen's) sexual organs. He became very badly frightened and left hastily. His fright persisted so that he was unable for years to bring himself to use a public toilet. Also he found it practically impossible thereafter to talk with anyone about any phase of sex. This inhibition was not overcome until he was past twenty years of age.

The three cases cited state briefly the influence of particular incidents or influences upon the sex adjustments of each boy. More frequently poor sexual adjustments are the product of a long history of influence by undesirable associates or circumstances. Often information is obtained from street corner gangs and in secretive ways. These sources are seldom reliable or accurate, and the attitudes they build are bad. On the other hand, an individual with satisfactory sexual adjustments may have had the good fortune to have a parent, brother, or older friend whose assistance over an extended period of time made adaptation to sexual urges a comparatively easy matter.

The next three cases are cited at length to give an idea how such influences operate and to show the effect of companions and environment. The first step in achieving proper adjustment is to get a clear understanding of the factors involved in the particular case. While David was fortunate in having the assistance of his brother, the difficulties met by Francis and William are not to their discredit. On the contrary they should be commended for realizing that a problem existed. Their experiences could be duplicated in many respects by hundreds of other boys.

David—Age 18. College student. Social adjustment excellent. Intellectually able, though scholastic record is average. Strongly interested in the promotion of social activities and other student projects.

At age eighteen, David is making a good adjustment so far as sex is concerned. He associates readily with both boys and girls. He goes regularly with a girl and they attend various college functions, finding a great deal of pleasure in each other's company. He experiences seminal emissions about three times monthly. He

[24]

feels normal physical urges, but no desires which make control troublesome or difficult. His associations with girls have always been on a high plane. To quote David, "Whenever I am with girls, I try to act like a gentleman." He does not practice masturbation and has never had intercourse.

The only time control of sexual urges was a problem was during David's first year in junior high school. At this time he matured sexually and for a while found considerable stimulation in associations with girls which involved a degree of intimacy. Kissing games at parties, dancing, and similar contacts were most likely to arouse excitation. The difficulty was not marked, however, and passed entirely when David entered senior high school and developed a number of absorbing interests.

Masturbation occurred from thirteen to fifteen years of age on the average of once a week. It practically always occurred after a party or some other exciting circumstance. David would return home with his mind on the incident and masturbate before going to sleep. It was done secretively, for he felt the practice was wrong and disliked it.

David feels that the chief assistance in his good adjustment has been the help given him by his brother, eight years his senior. Since David was twelve this brother has talked to him intimately and personally about problems of sex adjustment. When David was younger he did not discuss masturbation or sexual desires with his brother, yet in their conversations high ideals were upheld and specific suggestions were given which were of great assistance. The assistance still continues.

Francis—Age 22. College student. Above average intellectually and scholastically. Social adjustment very good. Leader in various activities. Interested in dramatics and athletics. Gives promise of fine professional career.

Francis has struggled for a number of years with the problem of masturbation. As a boy he led a somewhat sheltered life. His father ran a grocery store in a small town. When Francis was about twelve his father hired a young man, about eighteen, to assist with the clerking in the store, and since there was no other place for him to sleep, Francis was required to share his bed with the newcomer.

The first night the young man induced Francis to masturbate him. This was new to the boy and he was quite surprised when the seminal emission occurred. The significance of the proceedings was explained and Francis was told that he, too, would soon be mature since he already had a slight indication of pubic hair. The young man then masturbated Francis. This was repeated practically every night with a great deal of lascivious conversation. After about a year, the clerk was discharged but Francis was left with the habit of masturbation so firmly fixed that he has never overcome it, though the frequency has dropped from four or five times weekly to once a week.

The biggest battle has been to conquer the urgent desires aroused by the sexually stimulating conversations. The problem has been made easier by several good books and, most of all, by a friend of his own age whom Francis met when he was about sixteen. This boy became aware of Francis' problem when Francis once tried to masturbate him when they slept together. He, himself, was well adjusted because of the assistance

[26]

he had received from an understanding father. He had a strong influence over Francis and helped him to make a more satisfactory adjustment.

Francis has also been assisted in later years by an absorbing interest in his chosen field, biological science. This, together with the help of his friend, has been the chief factor in securing a good adjustment. Francis expressed bitterness over the failure of his parents to assist him by giving him sex instruction.

William—Age 23. College student. Excellent scholastic record. Very able in many types of activities. Participates in athletics. Holds positions of leadership, particularly as president of student body. Social adjustment very good. Well liked by both young people and elders.

William's introduction to sex came when financial necessity forced him to become a child laborer. One of his early jobs, secured when he was about eleven, was shining boots in a barber shop. Here, for the first time, he came into intimate contact with sex. Many persons loafed about the shop, and several of them became his sex teachers. They taught him masturbation and he continued it, usually indulging in it daily, for between two and three years. Never did he miss more than two days. He was told about intercourse, and urged to try to secure this relationship. The result was that at age fourteen he tried but failed. This simply aroused passions which led to another attempt which was successful.

At age seventeen, while he was in high school he met a young man who as coach and a fine physical specimen, quickly gained his deep admiration. Because of the coach's athletic prowess, this admiration became

[27]

hero worship. The coach learned of William's reputation and used his position as an excuse for talking with him.

This was the first reliable instruction William had received regarding sex. So strong was his confidence in the coach that he talked everything over with him, and found his attitude toward sex so changed that he decided to drop all efforts at sexual intercourse and "get straight." This he did in such a thorough fashion that he now looks back and marvels at how well it was done. He naturally feels a marked gratitude toward the coach for his help.

William has never stopped masturbation but now believes it does him no harm as a form of adjustment. He practices it about once a week. Sex desires and urges are felt occasionally but he has learned to handle them without difficulty. His social relationships with both sexes are carried on, on a high plane and are quite satisfactory socially, as well as to William as an individual.

Chapter III

FORMS OF SEX ADJUSTMENT

NUMEROUS REFERENCES have been made to forms of sex adjustment, but particular modes of behavior have not been discussed. This chapter will be devoted to a detailed description of the more common forms of adjustment and the conditions under which they are usually begun and practiced. An adjustment may be a consciously devised method of meeting the sex drive, or it may be a method which has been evolved without a conscious attempt on the part of the individual.

Two points should be kept in mind in reading this chapter. First, the classification of adjustments is made largely for purposes of clarity. Few persons have followed consistently any one of the forms mentioned here to the exclusion of all others. Most young men find themselves combining the various adjustments to meet their individual needs. Second, adjustments are sometimes changed or alternated quickly. One may adjust by masturbation for a period, drop it for a time, then follow with a period during which masturbation and intercourse are used interchangeably, then return to masturbation. While individuals may shift quickly from one type of adjustment to another, some changes are much more readily made than others.

[29]

The forms of adjustment most commonly used may be listed under four general headings. Each will be noted briefly, then followed by a more complete discussion

1. Complete sublimation refers to the direction of sex desires and urges into other interests and activities, Under this form of adjustment the individual would experience no direct sexual urges, nor feel an active interest in direct sexual satisfactions. Overt physical manifestations of sex would be nonexistent, or practically so. Partial sublimation, by arbitrary definition, refers to an adjustment in which the direct interests in sexual desires do not demand immediate physical outlets. Sexual interests exist but they are satisfied by finding an expression in other activities and friendly associations with other persons. The physical manifestations of sex are usually confined to occasional erections and involuntary seminal emissions.

2. The second form of adjustment is by the use of auto-erotic* practices. In this book only masturbation, the most commonly practiced form of auto-eroticism, is discussed.

3. Homosexual practices or other manifestations of sexual inversion in which the individual obtains sexual satisfactions from a member of the same sex represent a third form of adjustment.

4. Various forms of heterosexual contact may be used in making adjustment. Reference is made to the usual associations between young men and women, to petting and sexual intercourse.

* For a definition of auto-eroticism see page 40 or the glossary.

ADJUSTMENT BY PARTIAL SUBLIMATION

Many writers refer to the desirability of handling the sex drive by sublimation. This adjustment I have subdivided into two forms, complete sublimation and partial sublimation which I have defined as indicated above. Writers sometimes fail to make clear whether they refer to complete or partial sublimation. The word "sublimate" comes from the Latin and means "to raise above" or "be superior to." Theoretically this form of adjustment involves the redirection of sex energy into some form of absorbing interest.

Complete sublimation refers to a complete diversion of the sex drive into some such activity, for instance as the production of art, devotion to charity or some other high cultural or social good. Sex would be so utterly sublimated that no manifestation of it would occur even in the form of involuntary erections or seminal emissions. Students of sex psychology frequently express doubt concerning the ability or desirability of human beings to subdue and ignore sex drives so completely. In my own conversations, I have found not one individual who claims to have achieved this form of adjustment. Under modern conditions of living, with so many sources of sexual stimulation, there are good grounds for believing it impossible.

Partial sublimation is probably the form of adjustment to which most writers refer when they speak of sublimation. Partial sublimation is entirely consistent with a definite interest in sex when this interest is so directed as to make sex a positive contribution to the life of the individual and the well-being of society. This adaptation when used as a pre-marital adjustment becomes not negative but positive. Sex interests are recognized as normal and the issue is to direct them so that they give the maximum assistance in living happily.

As noted above, certain physical expressions of sex exist in partial sublimation. Probably the most frequent are erections. These are common to every male, though the frequency of occurrence varies widely from individual to individual and with the same individual. But erections are not always evidence of sexual excitation. They are very often experienced before arising in the morning as the result of pressure from a filled bladder which stimulates the nerve endings. Involuntary erections sometimes occur under other conditions. For example, several individuals report having erections while riding in automobiles, particularly when taking long trips. One needs also to realize that involuntary erections occur before the period of puberty.

Another important physical feature in adjustment by partial sublimation is the involuntary emission of semen during sleep, often known as a "wet dream." A concept which has recently been somewhat altered was that after semen was produced it was stored in the seminal vesicles, two pouches lying between the bladder and the testicles. These storage spaces were thought to become so filled with the semen that upon occasion their contents were automatically discharged at night. While this is still believed to be substantially true, there is increasing evidence to indicate that semen is secreted quite rapidly under mental stimulation. The so-called pressure of semen may be due in large measure to an accumulation created when mental preoccupation with sex is pronounced, rather than as the result of storage which has been regularly taking place over a period of time. Seminal emissions therefore may be a method of psychological as well as physiological adjustment.

In rare instances an individual making no use of masturbation or intercourse may experience no seminal emissions. A possible explanation is that a certain amount of seminal seepage carries off enough of the secretion to preclude emissions in the usual manner. Connected with this may be a slower rate of seminal secretion. This situation, while unusual, is not to be regarded as abnormal.

The case of a boy who first became a participant in this study at age twenty may be cited to illustrate this condition. He had never, so far as he knew, experienced a seminal emission, though he was in all respects quite normal physically except for his small stature. When about seventeen years of age he became associated with a group of boys who taught him to masturbate. Masturbation occurred over a period of eight months to a year with a frequency of two to three times a week. The usual orgasm and seminal emission occurred on such occasions, but between the ages of eighteen and twenty there were no emissions except for two or three times when masturbation was practiced. During this period the young man felt that he was entirely normal in his sexual desires, insofar as he was able to compare himself with others. He experienced erections and a desire for intercourse. He was keeping company with a girl whom he married at age twenty-one, and his sex adjustments after marriage followed a normal and satisfactory course.

The following case is especially interesting because it shows clearly the relationship that mental preoccupation and habitual patterns of behavior may have upon the frequency of seminal emissions.

Martin—Age 21. University student whose marks and ability are considerably above average. Has a wide variety of interests in cultural fields and travel. Held presidency of one college organization. Well-liked and highly respected by all associates.

Martin took up masturbation at sixteen. After practicing it for about a year, on the average of once or twice a week he attempted to stop but found it difficult. During this period seminal emissions occurred about twice a week. There was no evidence of ill health at the time. He was striving to break the habit of masturbation with a consequent state of worry concerning the mental ill-effects and the possible deleterious effects on the sex organs, and his seeming inability to conquer the habit. His mind was occupied with thinking about the habit itself and sex in general more during this period than usual. Later he returned to masturbation. During his twentieth year, he secured authentic information regarding sex adjustments which relieved any worries which might have persisted concerning the ill-effects of masturbation. The following summer Martin spent away from home working on a boat, an entirely new experience. His mind was constantly occupied with the new and interesting people and experiences which he was meeting. In this two-month interval masturbation occurred once and seminal emissions about every two weeks. After his return home, Martin was able to drop

[34]

masturbation to a frequency of about four or five times monthly.

Of the two frequencies for seminal emissions mentioned by Martin, the first and highest, twice a week, probably resulted from the struggle he was waging to stop masturbation. Being fearful of the possible ill-effects of the habit and fighting against it, his mind was more occupied with sex than before, and probably sexual stimulation without release of semen was a very frequent occurrence. The result was a constant secretion of seminal fluid which was disposed of by seminal emissions. This hypothesis is supported by the fact that later under different environmental circumstances and with a different mental attitude, the frequency of both seminal emissions and masturbation was lessened.

A number of studies have been made to learn whether any periodicity or definite regularity in seminal emission exists. No such period has been clearly established. Some individuals find emissions occurring with a certain degree of regularity about once every two or three weeks, while others find that for a long period none may occur, after which a number will cluster into a few days time.

Some young men are disturbed by dreams involving sexual conduct and desires at the time of emissions, feeling that sinister implications are involved. Such dreams are common, and occur in healthy, chaste individuals. The content of the dreams may vary widely from individual to individual and from dream to dream. They may involve women or girls in a sexual way, male sex organs, simple contacts between men and women, various parts of the body, images of masturbatory activities or inter-

[35]

course. Some individuals ask about the significance of male sex organs or the appearance of men in their dreams, feeling that this indicates sexual inversion or homosexual tendencies. There seems to be no foundation for this belief. Persons wholly normal in their heterosexual adjustment sometimes find such images appearing in their dreams.

Emissions may, of course, occur without dreams. In these cases the manifestation is in the form of an erection followed by emission. This sometimes takes place without the individual realizing it and may explain why some persons report that emissions occur very infrequently.

Nocturnal emissions, though occurring involuntarily, may be induced by numerous circumstances. These differ so much from individual to individual that no single causative circumstance can be listed. Pressure on the sex organs resulting from sleeping face downward, ·or from some other position or device may result in emissions. The state of the bladder upon retiring may also have an effect, a full bladder being more likely to induce them. Strenuous physical exercise, emotional excitement, or other stimulating circumstances may result in emissions, particularly if the stimulation or excitement is of a sexual nature and release is not otherwise secured. One young man who was a member of a band reported that music had the power of moving him emotionally and that a particularly thrilling concert served to induce seminal emissions. Certain foods, heavy eating before retiring, and excessive use of alcohol were mentioned by others as factors which they felt had a bearing on the frequency of emissions.

Other young men reported that fondling, petting, and other intimate heterosexual contacts tended to arouse stimulation which in turn induced "wet dreams." Other conditions which seemed to have some influence include such factors as exercise, mental imagery of a sexual nature, and situations which produce emotional strain. The period preceding a seminal emission, is for some a time during which they experience a feeling of abdominal tenseness and turgidity. At such times, if the discomfort is pronounced enough, it is logical to expect that measures will be taken to secure release. This may be secured in several ways. Some young men find it possible to exercise vigorously enough to relieve the discomfort, though this may be largely a mental release, while others resort to different methods, particularly to masturbation.

The ordering of the sex interests of the individual to achieve an adjustment by partial sublimation seems to depend upon a number of factors. One of the foremost influences is the conditions under which a person has been reared. If a boy is fortunate enough to have understanding parents or a competent adult advisor with whom he can speak frankly, the possibility of his making such an adjustment is decidedly increased. The case of Raymond indicates the kind of assistance which should be of great value in helping a youth to avoid sexual difficulties and worries.

Raymond—Age 20. Had very high marks in high school and college. A pre-law student. Esteemed by associates of both sexes, and by young and old alike. Has held various positions of leadership in the student body. Below average in athletic participation.

Since maturity Raymond has had an active interest in sex, though it has never been a pressing issue. From his early boyhood he has had the closest relations with his father, who at various times has given him instruction. As an illustration, at the time of puberty Raymond found that he frequently experienced a desire to see the nude female body. He told his father, and his father discussed the matter with him, explaining the anatomical differences between men and women, and other aspects of sex such as intercourse, prostitution, boy-girl relationships, and sexual control. Several conversations on sex took place between Raymond and his father, and these he feels gave him a very objective and wholesome point of view. This served to relieve his mental preoccupation with the female body, in general satisfied his questions, and established his faith in his father as a guide.

Raymond has never masturbated, nor had sexual relations. He has girl friends with whom he associates, having dates quite frequently. Seminal emissions occur about once a month.

Generalizations in regard to those who have adjusted by partial sublimation must be made on a very small number of cases. There is evidence that this method is infrequently followed, particularly if one limits its followers to those who have never made use of any other form of adaptation. Yet a number of young men are found who have made just such an adjustment.

If those who practiced masturbation for only a short

period and then used partial sublimation are included in the group, it is easier to note the factors involved. One of the most important of these is the development of deep and active interests in fields outside of sex. For example, if the individual is occupied with mechanical pursuits, reading, hiking, athletics, or has an absorbing hobby, the possibility of using partial sublimation is much enhanced. If, besides interest, the hobby gives a reasonable degree of physical activity, the achievement of a satisfactory adjustment, for some individuals at least, becomes still easier. Most of the young men who had maintained sexual adjustment by partial sublimation were actively participating in something of decided interest to them. The case of Alvin, described at length in the last chapter, is an excellent illustration of the beneficial effects of a good home environment and an absorbing interest.

Sound habits of eating and sleeping, sobriety, and personal cleanliness are also of assistance in adjusting by partial sublimation. The sexual organs are only one part of the human mechanism which as a whole operates according to definite physical laws. Improper habits of eating, improper exercise, or violations of any other fundamental rule of health result in physical maladjustments. These, in turn, influence sex adjustments. Plain but good foods supplying plenty of energy, enough sleep in a room with the correct temperature, and sufficient covering for warmth but no more, are important aids in achieving adjustment by partial sublimation. The use of alcohol, according to the statements of a number of young men, creates the problem of maintaining rational control over sex desires.

Physical cleanliness is essential. In bathing one should be careful to remove the grayish white substance, known as smegma, which accumulates between the foreskin and the head of the penis. This substance, produced by the sebaceous glands, is likely to cause an irritation which may result in sexual stimulation and masturbation. Proper wearing apparel is also important. Clothing which does not bind or irritate the sexual organs is particularly desirable.

Most important of all, to achieve an easy adjustment by partial sublimation, one should avoid using the more stimulating forms of adjustment and keep away from contacts which arouse sexual excitation. Individuals who have escaped masturbatory practices, or the arousal of lascivious desires by associates or environmental circumstances, and who, as they grew up, have had the information they needed, seem to find adjustment by partial sublimation simple and natural. It is much easier to make a good sexual adjustment to begin with than it is to correct a faulty one.

ADJUSTMENT BY MASTURBATORY PRACTICES

Masturbation is but one phase of a larger group of sexual practices commonly designated as auto-erotic. Auto-eroticism, as defined by Havelock Ellis,* "ranges from occasional voluptuous daydreams, in which the subject is entirely passive, to the perpetual unashamed

* Ellis, Havelock. *Studies in the Psychology of Sex.* Volume I, Part I, "Auto-Eroticism." New York: Random House. 1936. Page 162.

efforts at sexual self-manipulation witnessed among the insane. It also includes, though chiefly as curiosities, those cases in which individuals fall in love with themselves." Ellis also classifies the "sexual orgasm during sleep" as a typical form of auto-eroticism.

The larger field of auto-erotic practices is far too extensive and complex to fall within the scope of this book. Only the very common practice of masturbation, a form of adjustment used by both sexes, will be considered.

This practice has been long and widely known and strongly frowned upon. So much has been written about its baneful aspects that the truth has been difficult to find. There are, in particular, two points of view which should be noted: first, that masturbation is largely a phenomenon of childhood and early adolescence; and second, that the practice, if continued, will produce various dire effects. Recent investigations, including the studies for this volume, have tended to alter both these points of view.

The practice of masturbation is very prevalent. Few boys grow to manhood without having at some time masturbated, most of them for an extended period. Authorities vary in their estimates of the percentage of males who have at one time or another followed the practice, but that the estimate may be placed as high as ninety per cent seems certain.

In a study* made of 1029 North Carolina boys during 1920-21 Hughes found that "eighty-five per cent of the whole number reported that they had, at some time,

* Hughes, Walter L. "Sex Experiences of Boyhood." *Journal of Social Hygiene*. 12:262-273. May, 1926.

practiced masturbation." Similarly, Peck and Wells*
made a study of the sex history of almost 250 college
graduate men. In response to the question, "At what
age did you begin masturbation and how long did you
continue?" seventy-seven per cent answered in such a way
as to indicate the practice. Nine per cent of the answers
could not be classified, seven per cent of the group
omitted the question, and only seven out of every hundred denied masturbation.

Peterson† made a study of 419 college men. Of this
number only twenty-six, or 6.2 per cent, said they had
never masturbated.

Most writers assume that masturbation is a form of
adjustment found in late childhood and early adolescence, and in the majority of cases quickly left behind.
Actually it is neither a childhood nor an adolescent
phenomenon in the sense that it is confined to those
periods of life. Investigations are making this increasingly clear.

W. S. Taylor‡ in his report, "A Critique of Sublimation in Males," studied forty single men between the ages
of twenty-one and thirty-eight to find the form of sexual
adjustment which each was making. These men were
judged superior in scholastic ability, health, and character; all of them stood high in graduate and profes-

* Peck, M. W. and Wells, F. L. "On the Psycho-Sexuality of College
Graduate Men." *Mental Hygiene.* 7:697-714. October, 1923.
† Peterson, Kenneth M. *Early Sex Information and Its Influence on
Later Sex Concepts.* Boulder: University of Colorado. Unpublished
Master's thesis, 1938.
‡ Taylor, W. S. "A Critique of Sublimation in Males." *Genetic Psy-
chology Monographs.* January, 1933. Volume XIII.

sional schools in American universities. It is interesting to note that sixty-three per cent of them still maintained masturbation as a form of sexual adjustment. Peterson* in his study of college men found that forty-three per cent of those answering his question, "Do you now masturbate?" replied that they did.

Among the individuals with whom the author has discussed sex adjustment, slightly over sixty per cent were still practicing masturbation. The average age of this group, about twenty and one-half years, was less than that of Taylor's group, while the age range was from eighteen to twenty-five years. Again it becomes clear that masturbation is not a childish practice which is abandoned after a short period of use about the time of puberty. For a large proportion of young men this adjustment once made is continuous until it is replaced by some alternate adjustment, such as intercourse.

The average age at which boys begin masturbation is around fourteen to fifteen years though, as with other phenomena, the age range is wide. Several individuals report beginning as young as six to eight years of age. On the other hand, masturbation may begin several years after puberty. When it begins in the late teens or after the age of twenty it is probably consciously adopted to relieve tension and for pleasure in the experience. The case of Edward illustrates the use of the complete act of masturbation to release tension and secure pleasure.

> Edward—Age 24. College student. Above average scholastic ability. Actively interested in studying and writing about current social problems. Adjusts read-

* Peterson, Kenneth M., *op. cit.*

ily to both boy and girl friends. Health only average, having a heart somewhat weakened by childhood ailments. (Further history on page 129.)

Edward at age 19, had never completed masturbation or had sexual intercourse but he reported sexual desires of considerable intensity daily. These urges always occurred after awakening. He had the habit of lying in bed for fifteen or twenty minutes. During this time he experienced a strong erection and desire for sexual satisfaction. This stimulation was accompanied by mental pictures and phantasies of sexual intercourse. Masturbation was indulged in to the point of securing pleasurable sensations though Edward said he had never carried the act to completion.

Edward discussed this adjustment with the author and was advised to arise promptly upon awakening rather than waiting for the usual stimulation to occur. This advice he did not follow.

It was then suggested that if any harm was to result from masturbation, Edward was already experiencing it since he aroused a strong tension and then masturbated to the point of climax but secured no release. He thereupon decided to complete masturbation. For a time, masturbating about twice weekly, he felt this adjustment more satisfactory than the previous one.

Two years later he wrote that he felt his adjustment less satisfactory than at first. Masturbation occurred from two to four times weekly and he felt that this frequency left him so devoid of sexual desires that there was no real inclination to associate with girls in any except a perfunctory way. At the time he made this statement, a love affair with a girl for whom he had long cared had just broken up, and he was in-

[44]

clined to lay part of the blame on his prosaic and un-
romantic approach which he felt was in some degree
the result of masturbation. He expressed a belief that
he needed to use some other method of meeting his
sexual urges, or at least to lower the frequency of
masturbation.

About a year later he met a second girl for whom
he developed a strong affection. In this instance he
experienced no hesitancy or reticence in the relationship. Before the affair had continued long, intercourse
occurred, though Edward expressed considerable disappointment that the physical pleasure was not as
great as he had expected. The frequency of masturbation had not decreased before intercourse took place,
and Edward continued to use masturbation after intercourse began.

An analysis of Edward's adjustment is of considerable
interest. I am inclined to believe that his entire problem
was largely mental, the result of too constant preoccupation with sex. In his phantasies he had developed such
a strong desire for heterosexual relations that he could
not be content until he had the experience. Also he had
tended to idealize, one might say "deify," his first girl
friend in such a way that he could never bring himself
to be anything more than an awed admirer, worshipping
her from a distance. It was this attitude, rather
than the effects of masturbation, which kept him from
being more ardent. Later when he met the second girl,
he found no such inhibitions in expressing his affections. If my analysis is correct, and there are other factors not enumerated here to support it, what Edward
needed most was a change in his mental habits. His solu-

tion might have been first, abandoning the practice of masturbatory phantasies which constantly afforded both mental and physical stimulation; second, developing an engrossing interest to take the place of sex; and third, making a careful analysis of his attitudes, desires, and wishes in the field of sex to acquaint himself with the causes of his difficulties.

The conditions under which masturbation is begun vary. In a good many instances boys are taught by older companions. In some cases, it results from experimentation with the sex organs. Such experimentation may be brought about by curiosity aroused by conversations or reading, or as a result of watching an older individual, or by random manipulation of the sexual organs.

Masturbation often occurs for the first time when boys find themselves alone with nothing of interest to occupy them. A boy near the age of maturity often begins masturbation while lying in bed awake for long periods, or when he is in solitude, as in the bath or lavatory, for a long time. At this stage of life when the average boy is keenly aware of the increasing size of the sex organs, the appearance of pubic hair, and the other physiological changes which are taking place, it is very easy for him to begin manipulation and thus drift into masturbation.

Masturbation is particularly likely to take place during periods of solitude, or when the lack of clothing makes access to the organs easy. Conditions which raise bodily temperature considerably seem also to cause a degree of sex stimulation. Periods of time when pairs or even groups of boys are together without interesting activities or supervision, or when idleness hangs heavily on their hands often provide the opportunity for beginning masturbation. Over and over I have secured from young men clear proof that the type of companions with whom they associate often has a decisive influence upon the sex practices they follow. This is particularly true with respect to establishing the habit of masturbation. Younger boys are often taught by older boys, and boys the same age teach one another, especially when they are allowed to sleep together. Family servants, roomers and boarders, and other transients in or outside the home may serve to introduce children to undesirable practices.

Specific illustrations, such as the following, of the manner in which masturbation is begun might be cited endlessly. One boy went to work in the wheat fields where he met an older youth who gave him sex misinformation and taught him masturbation. A second boy learned from seeing members of a boy gang practicing it while undressed for swimming. He later tried it himself to see what it was like. Another boy left home to visit relatives and was given a bed upstairs across the hall from an older boy who was working for the family. After the family had retired the older boy came into his room to sleep with him, and showed him how to masturbate. After several similar incidents the boy came to practice it alone from daily to three or four times a week. A fourth boy took it up after reading a particularly stimulating account of sexual misconduct in a cheap, salacious magazine.

Another indication that free, unsupervised time and easy access to the sex organs facilitate masturbation is found by ascertaining the times at which the practice most frequently occurs.

By far the greatest number of instances occur at night before going to sleep or in the morning before rising. The young men taking part in this study indicated the first mentioned time more often but the difference was not great. Other times given were: when taking a warm bath or shower, after a particularly stimulating sex experience, when ill in bed, at times when tired, and at times when in solitude. A number of individuals mentioned masturbation as occurring in the company of another boy, but most of these instances took place in early adolescence. There were reports of such incidents at a later age but the occurrences were too infrequent to be classified as fixed homosexual practices.

The frequency of masturbation varies considerably. In early adolescence it is greater than in later adolescence and early youth. At the beginning of adolescence the frequency will usually vary from monthly to two or three times a week, but in some instances a frequency of once or twice daily is maintained. With older boys and young men it is most likely to range from once a week to two or three times a month.

The boy of fifteen who masturbates usually does so two or three times weekly. The frequency seems to be greatest when the habit is first begun. In a few cases boys have practiced it daily for rather long periods, and cases of even greater frequency are recorded by investigators. For one person coöperating in this study the frequency was two to three times daily for a short period. In this case the subject later took up normal sexual re-

[48]

lations with, so far as could be determined, no ill effects from his previous habits.

Various young men have remarked upon the difficulty of ceasing masturbation once the practice has been followed for any length of time. This difficulty seems to be greater if the individual struggles against it. One of the first rules in stopping masturbation is to avoid fighting blindly, and to discontinue worrying about its ill effects. A battle waged against the habit because of frantic, unreasoning fear is almost certainly doomed to failure. Boys trying to break the habit this way have found over and over again that the unwanted practice fastens itself upon them even more firmly. Such is not always the outcome, but it happens frequently enough to make plain that fights carried on under such conditions are usually futile.

Two cases, those of Arthur and Roget, are included to indicate the mental distress that often accompanies masturbation. The struggle they waged is typical of that carried on by many other individuals. The results, too, are typical.

> Arthur—Age 24. College graduate. Honor student. Chosen as member of honor societies. Marked intellectual ability. Outstanding as leader both in high school and college. Held many elective offices, a number of them presidencies. Interested in church activities. Member of athletic team. Very energetic. Very well liked. (Further history on page 101.)
>
> Arthur began masturbation at thirteen with an average frequency of once a week. He always felt extremely guilty concerning the practice. Many times

after masturbation, he felt so ashamed and angry that he inflicted punishment upon himself which often took the form of donning a track suit and running until physically exhausted. Sometimes prayer was resorted to, together with other devices, but he continued masturbation with a frequency of once or twice monthly. In the meantime, he began to study sex psychology and sex adjustments and came to realize that masturbation as an adjustment would cause him no particular harm. This understanding and the cessation of struggle eliminated his feeling of guilt. There has been no mental distress since, and masturbation now occurs very rarely.

Roget—Age 26. Health excellent. College graduate. Excellent character. Member of athletic teams, debate teams and many other school activities. Outstanding student in high school and college. Member of a number of honor societies. Social adjustment average. Marked intellectual ability. Well liked by young and older persons. Leader in various community activities. (Further history on page 136.)

Roget began masturbation at about age thirteen, practicing it from daily to ten times a week. He did not realize for some time what he was doing. Later he heard of the ill effects attributed to masturbation, realized he was practicing it, and began an almost frenzied struggle against it. He punished himself by allotting himself unusually hard physical tasks. He drew rings around dates on the calendar when masturbation last occurred, denied himself attendance at shows, wrote pledges to stop, frequented confessional, and otherwise struggled against the habit. He never succeeded in breaking it, but information gained from reading books on sex adjustments was of assistance in revising his attitude. He continued masturbation at twenty-five on the average of two or three times a week and expected to continue until marriage.

Roget commented, "I've never had anyone to whom I could talk about sex adjustment when I needed to. I've kept all of it to myself and managed to get it straightened out pretty well. People will never know the battle I've been through. I can still see the effects of it on myself."

The cases of Ellis and Vance further illustrate the beneficial effects of a change in attitude toward masturbation and the value of objective discussion in the matter of adjustment. Relieving the sense of shame and fear is one of the chief aids in cutting down the frequency of the practice.

Ellis—Age 21. University student. Marks average. Active worker with junior boys' organizations. Social adjustment average, somewhat withdrawing. Gets along well with associates.

Ellis began masturbation at the age of twelve after being initiated into the practice by friends. While he was never particularly worried about its harmful effects, he did feel that it was a shameful practice and wanted to break away from it. The frequency ranged from every other day to about twice weekly.

Ellis' father, evidently suspecting the difficulty, tried to talk with him about sex problems, but both were embarrassed and confused. As a result the conversation failed and Ellis was left more certain than ever that masturbation was a very despicable practice. His

[51]

first authentic information came from hearing a lecture on sex when he was twenty. At this time he received assurance that he was not harming himself, and that the correct mental attitude would help in coping with the habit. He accepted this point of view with the result that a year later the worry had ceased, and the frequency of masturbation had dropped to about twice monthly.

Vance—Age 19. College sophomore. Social adjustment good. Holder of various positions of leadership. Active in church work and young people's groups. Well liked by all associates.

Vance learned masturbation by experimentation at age fifteen and practiced it about twice weekly over a period of several years. His chief difficulty was extreme embarrassment regarding sex, particularly masturbation. When he had an opportunity to talk objectively with an adviser, he could not at first bring himself to do so. Later he had several long talks and found his embarrassment so relieved that he discussed the matter frankly. The problems of masturbation, after the talks, passed into the background and the frequency dropped markedly.

A good many of the young men who discussed their use of masturbation stated that it was to gain physical relief from sexual tension. As I became more familiar with individual problems of sex adjustment through direct conversations, the assumption that masturbation was a means of gaining physical relief broadened to the belief that, though it might afford this relief at times, the need for it was closely related to the sexual desires and attitudes of the individual, if not dependent upon

[52]

them. These desires and attitudes, in turn, seemed to be a part of the general environment in which the person lived. Therefore, if he could change his habitual ways of thinking and reacting to environmental influences, his masturbatory adjustment might change also. In other words, masturbation is a part of the individual's routine of everyday life.

If, then, his pattern of activity is changed, will a change in sexual behavior follow? In an effort to determine the answer to this question I have been fortunate in having the opportunity of following the adjustments of a number of individuals over a period of time. These individuals have coöperated by reporting their reactions.

Because it shows clearly the relationship of mental desires and habitual patterns of behavior to the practice of masturbation and general sexual adjustment, the case of James is especially interesting. The following account is the result of an analysis to which James subjected his own desires and feelings in regard to sex.

> James—Age 22. University student with a scholastic standing considerably above average. Reads widely, and is interested in music and other cultural activities. Active in extra-curricular activities. Highly respected for his integrity and well liked by all.

> James began masturbation at age sixteen and continued except for a short period at about age seventeen at which time a struggle to stop was given up as a failure. The average frequency was from once to twice a week. Masturbation was practiced largely for the pleasure it afforded. At age twenty, he spent the summer away from home. In new surroundings and

among new associates masturbation was dropped. But one instance occurred in three months and this was not due to any felt need. After James returned home, masturbation was resumed but at a rate of four to five times monthly. At that time James felt that masturbation was the result of a certain degree of irritability, feeling of abdominal discomfort, and an inability to concentrate on tasks. These symptoms were not pronounced. There was also some desire to experience the pleasurable effects.

During a subsequent summer, James was again away from his familiar surroundings. The summer's activities involved considerable travel and James found during the time he was traveling and was in the company of other persons there was little thought about sex. For over two months he roomed alone in strange surroundings. During the first few weeks masturbation occurred but once. After James began to get more accustomed to his situation he found the desire for masturbation growing and the frequency became as high as twice a week, which was greater than when he had been traveling or residing at the university fraternity and had the company of other young men. He was uncertain what caused the variation in the frequency of masturbation, but felt it might be due to lack of interesting associations, particularly with persons his own age.

In the fall he resumed his regular work at the university. He reported that the frequency of masturbation dropped to once every week or ten days. Masturbation nearly always occurred after retiring and before going to sleep. He reports that the more he studies his own adjustment the more he feels that masturbation results not so much from a feeling of abdominal tenseness or physical need as from the desire for pleasurable effects.

How much masturbation is practiced for pleasure is difficult to say. The pleasure element probably plays a much larger part than appears from an examination of the cases cited in this book. One reason for this is that many of the individuals reporting the use of masturbation wholly as a release from tension did so in good faith, but found it difficult to distinguish mental desires from physical urges. One individual agreed that he was "not averse" to the pleasure masturbation afforded, while another expressed the belief that nine out of ten use masturbation to some extent for pleasure. Several agreed that it played a considerable part.

A second case illustrating the influence of attitudes, habitual reactions and environmental circumstances is that of Otis. He began masturbation at about twelve years of age, practicing it three to four times weekly. Masturbation still continued at age twenty-two with a frequency of two to three times a week, though on several occasions Otis found the desire either forgotten or brought under control. When asked for a history of sexual adjustment which would make clear the effect which he felt environmental circumstances had had on masturbation, he wrote the following report based upon a diary he had kept.

> Otis—Age 22. College senior. Very much interested in English and actively engaged in writing. Social adjustment satisfactory. An exceptionally energetic individual.

"Age 13. September, 1927, I attended a 4-H Club camp at the State Fair. Here widely varied activities, trips, excursions, parties, and exhibits, claimed my attention. Frequency of masturbation had been at least every other day—and that attained only by a great deal of restraint. Yet, for about six days, I didn't even think of masturbation—at least not with desire to indulge. But on the night before departure, half asleep, I found myself masturbating again.

"June, 1931. Age 17. I spent a week at an Epworth League Institute camp. I was very much interested in activities and enjoyed the company of several girls. Morning erections upon awaking tempted me, but I held off masturbation for the entire week. I resumed the habit a few days after my return home.

"August-September, 1932. Age 18. At this time I was head over heels in love with first one, then another girl. For twenty odd days I gave myself and my chaotic feelings no relief other than that of automatic seminal emission.

"October, 1933. Age 19. After the finish of a clandestine love affair, in the effort to tie myself emotionally to something, I fixed upon the absent mistress as that object. To gratify myself by masturbation, I decided, would be unfaithful to my feeling for her. But continual thinking of the relationship, lately broken off, hardly reduced desire. I stuck it out a day or two more than a week, and for months afterward kept the frequency down to about three times in two weeks. I studied, read, and endeavored to write a great deal at this time, in addition to doing some work on the farm.

"December, 1936. Age 22. During the Christmas

vacation of twenty days a close friend and I decided upon a real adventure of hitch-hiking to Florida. We made the trip, had all the adventure we had antici- pated and more. During this period there was not a single instance of masturbation, nor any thought of it, though the frequency previous to the trip was two to three times weekly."

The experiences of James and Otis emphasize the marked assistance that new environment and associates and a change in interests offer in breaking away from the adjustment. Still another bit of evidence which in- dicates that masturbation is simply a part of a larger pattern of living is the frequency with which college and university men report the practice on week-ends. Release from the pressure of work while school is in session and freedom to stay late in bed presents an opportunity for masturbation which is habitually ac- cepted. Week-ends when this routine is upset mastur- bation is likely to be omitted, but upon the resumption of the customary activities it is also resumed.

For those interested in stopping the practice or de- creasing its frequency, the relationship between habit, routine, and mental attitude and masturbation makes it possible to offer two suggestions. First, the habit is most readily changed when a definite change of environ- ment takes place. The case of Neil given on page 191 of the last chapter shows the beneficial effects of such a change. Various persons have related similar experi- ences, though a return to the earlier environment is likely to result in a resumption of the earlier adjust- ment. Second, the physical tension which results in mas-

[57]

turbation is largely the outgrowth of a mental habit-uation toward the practice. Rather than a physical condition producing an awareness of a need for release, the situation more likely is something like this: the individual finds himself in the condition, place, or time at which masturbation usually occurs. He is aware of it, and whether actively conscious of it or not, his desire for sexual satisfaction is aroused. This gives rise to a feeling of physical tension which calls for release. For this reason, the way to change the habit is not to fight it, but to analyze the conditions under which it occurs and alter them.

Of course, masturbation may still provide a form of physical release after the tension has been aroused, regardless of the nature of its origin. That it is so used, at least with older boys, is evident. Several, in speaking of the drive which resulted in masturbation, said they were sure that they experienced a sense of tension in the abdominal region which caused them to seek release. Whether the tension was caused by mental desires and conditioning growing out of previous masturbatory habits, or by sexual stimulation from outside factors such as dates, movies, or companions, was not always clear even to the individual.

Some young men take a very matter-of-fact attitude toward the whole question and use masturbation simply as a form of quick escape from mental preoccupation with sex. For example, a college man, an outstanding leader on his campus, reported that he began masturbation shortly after sex maturity and used it continuously thereafter, though with a decreasing frequency. During his entire college career he masturbated on the average of two or three times a month when abdominal discomfort became too great or when mental preoccupation with sex disturbed concentration. To quote him, "I never sit around thinking about sex and women. When I feel a strong sexual urge coming on I masturbate, and eject the semen with the same attitude that I might use in disposing of bodily waste."

In literature relating to sex adjustment constant warnings are issued against the physical and mental ill effects resulting from excessive masturbation. Just what constitutes excessive frequency is hard to decide. Havelock Ellis* implies that it is difficult to practice masturbation excessively if one's health is good. There is no criterion by which one is able to determine what constitutes excessive frequency, but such evidence as exists makes it seem improbable that any young man who is at all normal, physically and mentally, will harm himself permanently by masturbation. Constant handling of the penis, such as would be necessary in masturbating two or three times daily, is likely to produce in most persons a condition of soreness which would make this frequency impossible. Ellis† cites from the writings of another author a case defined as excessive in which the young man practiced the habit daily or twice daily from eight to ten years.

Both physical and mental degeneracy have been suggested as results of masturbation. No evidence is avail-

* Ellis, Havelock. *Studies in the Psychology of Sex.* Vol. I, Part I, "Auto-Eroticism." New York:Random House. 1936. Pages 250-251.
† Ellis, Havelock, op. cit.

able to substantiate these assertions. There is no indication that healthy individuals suffer lasting injurious physical or mental effects from the practice of masturbation itself, even when the frequency is as high as three or four times a week or even daily. The fact that so many young men continue to masturbate, and yet are splendid specimens of physical manhood is strong evidence that the practice does not have the evil effects frequently attributed to it.

The following case illustrates a high frequency of masturbation with no apparent ill effect physically or with respect to heterosexual adjustments. It also illustrates the procedures used in altering the frequency.

> Harris—Age 25. University student. Marks below average. Member of basketball team. Widely traveled. Well liked by members of both sexes.
>
> Harris began masturbation at about ten or eleven. The frequency was high—at least once a day—from the beginning. For a long time it was twice daily, morning and night. At age seventeen the first instance of intercourse occurred. Harris did not seek the experience but was introduced to it by an older person. After this promiscuous sexual relationships were alternated with masturbation, one or the other occurring several times weekly. At age twenty-three Harris became engaged and intercourse thereafter was confined to his fiancée. When not having intercourse regularly, masturbation occurred as often as three or four times weekly at age twenty-five. Harris was vigorous and physically active and felt that there were no physical ill effects from his sexual practices. Throughout this period he was constantly engaged in vigorous physical

activities, including competitive sports both in high school and college.

Despite his promiscuity, Harris had very little reliable information about sex matters, and felt that he was unique in his masturbatory adjustment. His desire for correct information led to a long discussion of the various forms of adjustment and a wish to make the best possible adaptation. About four months later, he reported that by mutual agreement with his fiancée, only two or three instances of intercourse had occurred in the interval. Similarly the frequency of masturbation had dropped to two or three times monthly. Later, during a summer vacation, Harris was engaged in interesting physical activities in a camp. Each evening found him so tired physically that sleep came as soon as he retired. During the entire summer masturbation occurred twice.

The real danger to physical or mental health from masturbation centers about the belief that one who practices it has fallen into the toils of a vicious habit. The worry which results, rather than the physical effects, does the harm. If the worry is intense enough there is no doubt that both physical and mental harm can result. Psychological case histories have, in numerous instances, pointed to the deleterious effects of anxiety caused by masturbation.

While serious danger of permanent physical and mental ill effects arising from masturbation may be heavily discounted with the normally adjusted young man, danger may arise from several other sources. Probably the habit could be so practiced as to produce a temporary condition of lassitude or languor. The case of Edward cited on page 43 may be an illustration of this. The sexual practice in which he indulged daily, provided ten or fifteen minutes of rather intense stimulation. It seems reasonable that the procedure he followed would have a much more weakening effect than actual masturbation carried to a climax quickly. Edward spoke often of a general "fagged-out" feeling, but this was so tied up with other health conditions which were definitely not connected with sex that it would be impossible to determine whether this feeling was wholly or in part the result of masturbation. A cause and effect relationship in such a case is difficult to determine.

Another possible undesirable result is that masturbation may be accepted as a full and permanently satisfying form of sexual adjustment. When this is the case, it usually is accompanied by withdrawing, unsocial behavior, which means that the individual may have centered his normal sex desires and urges on himself. If this occurs the readiness to accept this form of sexual gratification may interfere with establishing friendships with girls which may eventually culminate in marriage and normal heterosexual relationships.

This is probably an over-simplification of the matter. Acceptance of masturbation as a permanent form of sexual adjustment, coupled with retiring, unsocial behavior, one may strongly suspect, is symptomatic of deeper and more far-reaching difficulties. Both masturbation and the reserved behavior represent a sort of flight from reality and the individual who finds that he cannot make satisfactory adjustments in a normal way, resorts to them as escape devices. In such a case, before masturbation can be satisfactorily controlled, the individual must be helped in making satisfactory social adjustments. Masturbation is only one aspect of a much broader problem. It would be a harmful adjustment, not because of its physiological effects, but because the individual is using it to adjust without making the social contacts which one must normally have if he is to live satisfactorily.

Uncertainty is sometimes expressed concerning the effect of masturbation on normal marriage adjustments. The assertion is sometimes made that the practice may lead to impotence or premature ejaculation during sexual intercourse. This statement may be answered by the observation that many persons who have masturbated somewhat extensively have later made successful adjustments in heterosexual relationships.

There is no definite scientific answer to the question, though one writer* who has made as careful study as any available, frankly disagrees with the contention that sexual adjustments in marriage are adversely affected by masturbation and cites cases of both good and bad adjustment following a long history of masturbatory practice before marriage.

Nevertheless, some points on the other side should be presented. Havelock Ellis† writes: "In many cases it has seemed that masturbation, when practiced in excess, especially if begun before the age of puberty, leads to an inaptitude for coitus, as well as an indifference to it,

* Dickinson, R. L., in *Sex Life of the Unmarried Adult.* I. S. Wile, Editor. New York: Vanguard Press, 1933.

† Ellis, Havelock. *Studies in the Psychology of Sex.* Vol. I, Part I. "Auto-Eroticism." New York: Random House. 1936. Page 261.

[63]

and sometimes to an undue sexual irritability, involving premature emission and practical impotence. This is, however, the exception, especially if the practice was not begun until after puberty."

Even in this statement it will be noted that Ellis makes four qualifications. He is not sure that such is the case, masturbation must be practiced in excess, and in most instances be begun before puberty, and if an inaptitude for sexual intercourse does occur it is the exception. One might suspect that if, after all these qualifications, such a disability does appear it might easily be the result of something other than an excess of masturbation.

Little evidence was secured from the young men with whom I talked as to the effect of masturbation upon sexual adjustment in married life. Several of those reporting intercourse felt their experience had been normal and that previous masturbatory practices had had no effect so far as the ability and desire to carry on intercourse was concerned.

The individual reporting the longest period and highest frequency of masturbation reported at the same time several periods of some length when intercourse was used as a form of adjustment. Asked specifically if he felt that masturbation had made heterosexual adjustments difficult or in any way unsatisfactory he said he could see no such effect. So far as he could determine his heterosexual relations had been normal and natural. The case of Harris, on page 60, indicates the same condition.

A variety of reactions to the use of masturbation as a form of adjustment was received in talking with individual young men. Most of the persons using it have

[64]

believed it, at least to begin with, a harmful practice. With this background in mind, it is interesting to note that in so many cases they have observed no harmful effects in their own adjustments.

No individual coöperating in this study assumed masturbation to be the most satisfactory adjustment, though a number of them had accepted it as a solution to their present problems. As one young man, president of the college Y.M.C.A., age twenty-two, remarked, "I feel sure it doesn't hurt me. It helps me achieve control and it is the method I intend to use until I marry."

Other individuals expressed the belief that masturbation was the best adjustment outside of marriage since it is a method of control readily available to the individual. Those expressing dissatisfaction usually did so because of uncertainty as to the mental effects of masturbation, aesthetic disapproval of the habit, or because of the desire for heterosexual adjustment. Only one expressed dissatisfaction because he was uncertain about physical effects.

Measures for controlling masturbation are briefly discussed below under two classifications, (1) preventive, (2) moderative (including stopping altogether). These measures rise naturally and directly out of the preceding discussion of masturbatory practice.

The following preventive measures are, of course, designed to keep masturbation from being taken up as an adjustment. Briefly stated they are:

1. Learn good physical habits. This includes plenty of active outdoor exercise. Good, plain, substantial foods should constitute the diet.

[65]

2. Form the habit of retiring when ready to sleep and arising at once when awake. Your sleeping room should be at least moderately cool. The mattress should be fairly hard. Use enough covers to keep warm, but not too warm.

3. Keep busy with interesting things. Avoid periods of solitude with little or nothing to do.

4. If possible, select desirable companions; those who will assist you by providing a variety of other interests.

5. Secure enough information about your own body and about sex adjustments to understand clearly what is desirable and undesirable.

6. Achieve an attitude which helps you to look upon sex without confusion or embarrassment. Think of it as an expression of a normal human drive.

If the problem is one of moderating or stopping masturbation once it has been started, each of the preceding suggestions will apply. In addition these should be added:

1. Avoid worry and distress. Fighting the habit frantically is likely to intensify the difficulty.

2. Select, if possible, someone with whom you can discuss the matter freely. It will help simply to talk the problem over with some competent, understanding person.

3. Avoid situations in which excessive stimulation and excitation are apt to occur.

4. Study the conditions under which sexual arousal takes place and determine for yourself what measures will be most helpful in properly controlling such arousal.

Little emphasis has been laid on the harmful effects of masturbation, but this is not to be interpreted as approval of this form of adjustment. Certainly a young man who has been adjusting successfully by partial sublimation should not be advised to start masturbation. While it is my position that no harmful effects, beyond possible worry, will result from the practice, I do not intend to encourage the formation of a habit which has been so long under suspicion and is so widely disparaged. Perhaps there are undesirable effects which I have over-looked. In any event, my desire is not to start others following it, but to allay the fears of those already using masturbation as a form of adjustment—and this, incidentally, is one of the best ways to combat the practice. There has been so much anxiety caused by misconceptions concerning the effects of masturbation, and so many futile, harmful struggles waged against the habit that it seems important to set forth the facts so far as they are known.

Let us assume masturbation practiced by a normally healthy boy, who is at the same time making social adjustments readily to both boy and girl friends. Unless he is worrying about the practice, there is no scientific evidence which I have been able to find which indicates that the results will be harmful. The boy should be made aware of all the issues involved, but not alarmed; and should be assisted in making such adjustment as he and his adviser think desirable. A careful analysis should be made to see that none of the possible harmful effects which have been noted exist.

Willoughby* reviewed various European and American studies on the subject of masturbation, and came to

* Willoughby, Raymond R. *Sexuality in the Second Decade.* Washington, D. C.: Society for Research in Child Development. Vol. II, No. 3, Serial No. 10. 1937.

four conclusions, based upon his summarization of the information in the studies. These conclusions were:

1. Self-gratification is the typical sexual behavior of early and middle adolescence, though practiced more commonly by boys than girls.

2. Auto-sexuality is largely a repression phenomenon resulting from enforced lack of opportunities for heterosexual associations.

3. No very satisfactory evidence exists to show any deleterious effects of auto-sexuality in adolescence or elsewhere.

4. There is some evidence that auto-sexuality is symptomatic of a withdrawing type of personality adjustment. Presumably it is practiced because of its availability as a means of satisfaction when, due to culture or environmental conditions, normal heterosexual outlets are difficult to find.

Three quotations from the works of Havelock Ellis* are included in an effort to bring the threads of the discussion together and show the general conclusions. These quotations should be studied carefully to note the conditions assumed in speaking of certain effects and the qualifications suggested in drawing conclusions.

"How far masturbation in moderately healthy persons living without normal sexual relationships may be considered normal is a difficult question only to be decided with reference to individual cases. As a general rule, when only practiced at rare intervals, and *faute de mieux* [for want of better] in order to obtain relief for physical oppression and mental obsession, it may be re-

* Ellis, Havelock, op. cit. Page 268.

garded as the often inevitable result of the unnatural circumstances of our civilized social life."

"While we may thus dismiss the extravagant views widely held during the past century, concerning the awful effects of masturbation, as due to ignorance and false tradition it must be pointed out that, even in healthy or moderately healthy individuals, any excess in solitary self-excitement may still produce results which, though slight, are yet harmful. The skin, digestion, and circulation may all be disordered; headache and neuralgia may occur; and, as in normal sexual excess or in undue frequency of sexual excitement during sleep, there is a certain general lowering of nervous tone."*

"It must always be remembered, however, that, while the practice of masturbation may be harmful in its consequences, it is also, in the absence of normal sexual relationships, frequently not without good results. In the medical literature of the last hundred years a number of cases have been incidentally recorded in which the patients found masturbation beneficial, and such cases might certainly have been enormously increased if there had been any open-eyed desire to discover them."†

ADJUSTMENT BY HOMOSEXUAL PRACTICES

The third form of adjustment mentioned at the beginning of this chapter included homosexual practices and other forms of inversion. Inversion is a less inclusive

* Ellis, Havelock, op. cit. Page 259.
† Ellis, Havelock, op. cit. Pages 268-269.

term than homosexuality, referring, according to Havelock Ellis, to any instance of the sexual instinct being turned by an inborn condition toward persons of the same sex. Homosexuality includes all sexual attractions between persons of the same sex, whatever the conditions causing the manifestation.

Terman and Miles define a homosexual as a person who, out of preference, has sexual relationships with persons of the same rather than the other sex.* Both male and female homosexuals are found, but the present discussion will be confined to males.

Homosexuality as a form of adjustment is practiced in varying degrees. If ample data were available probably they would show that a fairly large proportion of people have at some time or another felt a sexual attraction for one of their own sex. A large number of individuals begin their sexual activities by participation with a person of the same sex. Support for this statement can be found in some of the case studies in this book. A person may have, for the most part, all the attributes of heterosexual adjustment, yet occasionally find satisfaction in certain forms of sexual association with members of the same sex. The most pronounced cases are those of individuals who are so definitely homosexual that they can find no other sexual satisfactions. There are, then, differing intensities of homosexual feeling.

The causes of homosexuality are not fully known. The relative influence of heredity and environment is a much

* Terman, Lewis M. and Miles, Catherine Cox. *Sex and Personality.* New York: McGraw-Hill Book Co. 1936.

debated issue. Havelock Ellis,* one of the foremost students of the psychology of sex, feels that there must be at least a predisposing condition resulting from inherited conditions. That is to say, homosexuality itself is not inherited, but certain factors may be present at birth which give ready rise to it if the proper circumstances exist.

The three most common circumstances which, according to Ellis, afford an opportunity for the development of a latent tendency to homosexuality are: (1) the practice of homosexual play learned by actual participation in such activities with associates, (2) the seduction of a youth by older homosexuals, and (3) disappointment in love.

That there are many who participate in homosexual activities without becoming confirmed homosexuals is recognized, but for others it may serve as the entering wedge for this form of adjustment. A disappointment in love may leave the latent homosexual so disgusted with his experiences in the heterosexual field that he turns to association with his own sex for satisfaction.

Other authorities emphasize the importance of environmental influences in the development of homosexual adjustments. Terman and Miles in a recent study divided homosexuals into two classes, active and passive. Passive homosexuals are those who accept the feminine rôle and do so perhaps because of inherited characteristics. The active homosexuals are the aggressors

* Ellis, Havelock. *Studies in the Psychology of Sex.* Vol. II, Part II, "Sexual Inversion." Chapter VI. New York:Random House, 1936. Pp. 322-324.

[71]

in initiating sexual relations. With the latter group Terman and Miles* felt there was some evidence of environmental influences. They write:

"If the case-history data supplied by these individuals (eighteen in number) can be accepted as anywhere near the truth the psychological formula for developing homosexuality in boys would seem to run somewhat as follows: too demonstrative affection from an excessively emotional mother, especially in the case of a first, last, or only child; a father who is unsympathetic, autocratic, brutal, much away from home, or deceased; treatment of the child as a girl, coupled with a lack of encouragement or opportunity to associate with boys and take part in the rougher masculine activities; overemphasis of neatness, niceness and spirituality; lack of vigilance against the danger of seduction by older homosexual males. The formula of course does not always work. Doubtless many children who grow up in an environment of the kind just described become nevertheless heterosexual; possibly a majority do. In some of these cases the heterosexual adjustment is made only with difficulty; the man may have little interest in sex, he may select a wife much older than himself (a mother surrogate), or if he marries a younger woman she may find it impossible to win first place in his affections."

Some of the evidences of homosexual tendencies include an undue interest in the sex organs of others, a desire to fondle or pet members of the same sex, and an over-readiness to raise sexual topics of conversation, espe-

* Terman, Lewis M., and Miles, Catherine Cox. *Sex and Personality.* New York: McGraw-Hill Book Co. 1936. Pp. 319-320.

cially those relating to the sexual organs and sexual adjustments of others. But one must guard against letting a single instance of such behavior label another as having homosexual tendencies.

Further, it is important to remember that after having exhibited such tendencies, one is not necessarily homosexual forever after. "To have some homosexual experiences does not constitute homosexuality in the narrow sense; a homosexual act in itself does not stamp one as a homosexual."* A common attitude was expressed by a young man who stated that if he found that any friend of his, no matter how much he had cared for him, had ever indulged in masturbation with another boy he would drop him at once. He believed that homosexual practice was ineradicable and that anyone making use of it in any form was to be shunned as a pervert. But homosexuality is in fact not an unalterable, mysterious phenomenon which occurs in markedly abnormal behavior or not at all. It varies in the extent to which it is practiced and in the forms in which it is manifested.

Few instances of homosexuality were found among the cases investigated for this book, and all but ten or twelve of the incidents reported occurred near the time of puberty. All of the contacts were of short duration and showed little indication of becoming permanent adjustments. Many were the result of experimentation by boys reaching maturity and interested in finding out all they could about the entire field of sex. Lacking adequate information and finding idle time at hand this

* Brill, A. A. *The Psychiatric Approach to the Problem of Homosexuality.* The Journal-Lancet. 55:249-52, April 15, 1935.

interest is often expressed through experimentation in pairs or in groups.

Such experimentation may take the form of examination, comparison, or fondling of the sex organs, play at masturbation or intercourse, or various other ways. These manifestations, when they occur, should be regarded as evidence of a need for adequate and satisfying sex information, not as symptoms of unalterable perversion. Unless some rather serious circumstances surround a particular instance, the difficulty can usually be eliminated by adequate information and guidance. The persons involved should not be made to feel that they have committed an unpardonable sin, nor that their conduct marks them as perverted or debauched. Such an attitude is likely to make the difficulty even more pronounced.

Another factor which is apt to induce sexual play is the feeling of pleasure which comes from stimulating the sensitive zones around the sexual organs. These areas, known as erogenous zones, afford pleasurable sensations when caressed or when pressure is exerted on them, and without doubt this induces some individuals to indulge in the practice. A continuation of this adjustment over a period of time might lead to a permanent homosexual adjustment, though, as has been indicated, the genesis of homosexuality is not clearly known.

Instances of homosexual practices occurring among groups of heterosexually adjusted young men are often found when they are brought together under circumstances which make the usual methods of sexual adjustment impossible. Cases of homosexuality in non-coeducational schools, prisons, armies, navies, and other

[74]

situations in which members of a single sex are isolated are often mentioned in literature on sexual problems. Undoubtedly a great many of the participants are normal people who are seeking a sexual outlet. The manifestation most frequently found is that of mutual masturbation.

All instances of homosexual adjustment reported during the investigation for this book occurred in late adolescence or early manhood. All were instances of mutual masturbation. Nothing more is indicated by them than that the associations were established for the pleasure obtained from sexual stimulation by some other person. Those involved usually felt that sharp social disapproval was attached to actions of this nature, and they usually related their experiences with some degree of hesitation.

The feeling of social disapproval in regard to homosexuality may have been so strong that individuals who reported homosexual practices were not entirely frank, and that others who had participated in such experiences did not report them. Certainly society has set up sterner prohibitions regarding this form of adjustment than almost any other.

Homosexuality does make for much individual difficulty in social adjustment. The important thing is to be able to distinguish between the transitory type of homosexual contact based upon a desire to experiment or experience the generally pleasurable sensations resulting from erogenous stimulation, and the type of homosexuality (apt to be permanent), which is based upon an active pleasure in sexual contacts with members of the same sex, accompanied by a feeling of disinterest or even of displeasure, for contacts with members of the other sex.

Other forms of inversion besides those mentioned sometimes occur. They are found rather infrequently, however, and an enumeration of their specific manifestations is beyond the scope of this discussion. The reader who is interested is referred to the more elaborate treatises of sex and to books on abnormal psychology.

There are certain statements made relating to the common physical types found among homosexuals, and to the physical characteristics which are said to distinguish such persons. A prevalent belief is that young men who are slender, light-complexioned, or lacking in beard —those, in short, whose physique does not indicate a high degree of masculinity—are more likely to exhibit homosexuality or be susceptible to approach from homosexuals than others. While a few experiences can be offered to support this idea, it is at best a hypothesis. Further evidence is needed before any generalization can be made. Scientific proof of the association of homosexuality with these characteristics is lacking.

Young men should, however, know something of the manifestations of homosexuality. Individuals who are pronouncedly homosexual are often found in places where large numbers of people congregate, such as at railway stations, on street corners, in parks, at hotels and rooming houses kept for one sex only; in movies and theatres, or on trains or other vehicles. Since hitch-hiking has become such a common practice, it has provided another way of being approached by homosexual per-

[76]

sons. Several young men report being picked up by motorists who then made homosexual advances. They often make their contacts with individuals at such places, or under conditions when privacy seems assured, and a young man, particularly if unaccompanied, may find himself accosted. If he is aware of this possibility and knows something of the manifestations of homosexuality it should not be hard for him to distinguish the behavior of a homosexual from that of a stranger who is simply exhibiting a friendly interest.

The two cases which follow illustrate the way in which homosexual advances are sometimes made. Donald's information has been left in the first person so that it might be given as he wrote it.

> Donald—Age 26. Graduate student. Well liked by associates. Employed as teacher in public high school. Aggressive in his work and readily accepted professionally.

> "When I was ten years of age a man forty-five years old came to work for my father. He was unmarried, had a fine personality, and was highly respected by his associates. He became a very close personal friend of my entire family and his judgment to this day is respected, particularly by my father.

> "This man immediately became attached to me. I had played at having sex relations with a little girl before this, but had not experienced any form of masturbation. While riding alone with him one day he exposed my sex organs. An erection was immediate and he began manipulation. I was a little surprised but the experience was very pleasing. No climax was

reached. Then he took me into his complete confidence and told me that I shouldn't tell. The confidence was kept to the letter and would probably not
now be revealed except for scientific purposes. A few
days later in a similar setting a climax was reached.
On this occasion he maneuvered my hand to his sex
organs. This was particularly distasteful to me but I
probably submitted out of kindness to him. This part
of the bargain was revolting and remained so.

"The homosexual relations continued during the
summer that he worked for my father. They later continued when he would visit our home, or when I
would go to stay with him during a school vacation.
On one occasion while a sophomore in high school, a
boy friend of mine (with whom I had practiced mutual masturbation) went with me to spend a week-end
with this man. During the night the three of us experienced mutual masturbation. On two occasions
when I was visiting him alone we experienced homosexual intercourse. He was the active partner and I
the passive member of the relationship. Both would
have emissions. These experiences left an extremely
depressed feeling. I did everything to prevent this intimacy in the future. It was attempted on a later occasion but was unsuccessful.

"The mutual masturbation continued until I graduated from high school and on one occasion when I
was a freshman in college. Since then our relationships
have been merely hasty greetings when he visits our
home. On visiting him I have always managed to have
one or two friends with me, and then not to stay over-
night. I still enjoy seeing him and have been practically able to drive the homosexual practices from my

[78]

mind. I later, at the age of 21, experienced intercourse with prostitutes on several different occasions. One reason was that I was associated with a group, and because they were going to prostitutes, I did also. A second reason was that I wanted to convince myself that I could be normally heterosexual. During adolescence the relations did cause me much anxiety at times and resulted in much day-dreaming and very poor grades in my sophomore year in high school.

"As I look back on the experience it seems that excellent home training was the only thing which prevented me from developing homosexual tendencies later in life. These tendencies may also have been counteracted by the fact that my sister and I were always very close."

Calvin—Age 18. Average mental ability. Scholastic record above average. Social adjustment fair. Very quiet and reserved. Engaged to be married. High school graduate.

About age fifteen Calvin was introduced to homosexual practices by a man about twenty-eight or thirty. This man professed to be a spiritualist medium and had met Calvin and his mother several times in this capacity. After they had visited his apartment several times he urged Calvin to come alone for a further talk about spiritualism. Calvin consented.

When he made the visit, the spiritualist informed him that part of the rites in this particular sect involved complete disrobing on the part of both. Then Calvin was induced to submit to masturbation and to masturbate his seductor in turn. Calvin felt that the whole thing was wrong. He had had implicit confidence in the man to begin with, however, and having once started the incident, felt he could not stop. Calvin never returned to the spiritualist. There were no ill-effects from the experience.

One of the major problems is the attitude which should be assumed toward homosexual behavior. The common belief, as already noted, is that homosexuality is a loathsome and hideous phenomenon resulting from a perverted and ignoble mind. Actually it may be the product of environment, or as some think, the penalty assessed by a defective heredity.

Whatever the cause, those who are helpless against or ignorant of the invert and his adjustment must be protected against him. It seems best to think of homosexuality as a departure from the usual type of adjustment, and to seek to prevent its spread to those who may be injured by it. The confirmed homosexual should not be regarded as a pariah, to be destroyed if possible, but as one whose environment and heredity has involved him in an unfortunate adjustment which, in all probability, will prevent him from making heterosexual contacts satisfactory enough to warrant entering marriage and establishing a family.

ADJUSTMENT BY HETEROSEXUAL CONTACTS

Heterosexual contacts of varying degrees of intimacy form the last of the four methods of adjustment mentioned at the beginning of this chapter. These contacts may range from the day-by-day associations of young men and women in the classroom and at school parties and other functions, to intercourse.

Occasionally one meets individuals who have never

manifested an interest in heterosexual contacts. Such men may be aware of women as impersonal objects in their background but there is little or no sexual feeling involved.

Cord—Age 19. University sophomore. Well adjusted to male acquaintances. Academically successful. Above average intellect. Physically very active and vigorous.

Cord has always made his social adjustments satisfactorily in that he has been well liked by both boy and girl associates. He is not shy or withdrawing, but he has never had a date. He meets girls normally in the regular university activities, though any interest he may take in them is casual, transitory, and impersonal. He has had the usual contacts with girls all his life and has a sister four years younger.

An extended discussion was carried on to find the reason for Cord's attitude toward the other sex. While the cause could not be positively ascertained, it was found that when his sister was born he had had a temper tantrum and developed a marked antipathy for her. Until her birth he had occupied the position of importance in the household. Suddenly he found himself displaced by his sister, for whose coming he was totally unprepared. Out of this experience he may have formed the concept that the function of girls was chiefly to interfere with the pleasures of the male, and so he would have nothing to do with them. He appeared quite suspicious of girls and their motives, describing a situation in which a girl had indicated she would like a date with him. Cord turned her down because he felt she was "playing me for a sucker." He also expressed resentment against girls because they

[81]

had broken up several intimate friendships he had had with other boys. He also expressed the belief that girls couldn't do anything because they were too weak physically.

Cord's chief question, though he does not regard it as a worry, is whether he will ever develop enough interest in girls to marry. He has a number of active interests, particularly travel and work, and all his time is taken in their pursuit.

At present there is little scientific data available in regard to such adjustments, but the probability is that in most cases the heterosexual interest has never developed because of competing interests or lack of opportunity. For such individuals the utilization of opportunities for association with girls might serve to develop hetero-sexual interests. Yet Cord had some associations of this nature and found no real interest developing. Normally, however, one would expect such interest to develop slowly. The explanation centering about his antipathy for his sister may be an over-simplification, but the incident seems to have a bearing on his adjustment. About all that can be said now is that more scientific information is needed in regard to such adjustments.

About the time of puberty or within a few years afterwards most boys experience a growing interest in members of the other sex. Sometimes this is not outwardly evident, even in individuals who are strongly preoccupied with sex. Sometimes the mind is pervaded with ideas of sex in general, at others the preoccupation is with a particular girl.

For a while the interest in girls may be satisfied by

[82]

associations in the classroom, at parties and other functions, but most boys soon go beyond casual relationships and give their attention to one girl with whom they may keep company for a long time. The intimacy of this association may vary from simple friendliness to passionate love.

Interest in heterosexual contacts is normal and desirable. Only when it becomes an extreme preoccupation is it necessary to develop a wider range of activities to round out and maintain a more balanced social program. New occupations, new hobbies, many associations with other persons based upon non-sexual interests, and the avoidance of sexually stimulating factors will help in developing a wholesome attitude toward sexual conduct.

One of the sexually stimulating factors which leads toward greater intimacy is petting. Petting in this discussion is defined as physical intimacy between a boy and girl which results in or affords a means of physical sex stimulation. Petting often follows when couples permit their relationships to bring them into close bodily contact for a period of time.

Many young men use this adjustment as an outlet for the sex drive. Sometimes petting induces so much stimulation that seminal emissions follow during sleep. Sometimes it is carried so far that ejaculation occurs during petting. The difficulty is to stop short of intercourse. The extent to which one can go and still abstain from intercourse varies from individual to individual and situation to situation but evidence shows that the chances are against going only part way, then stopping.

[83]

In a study by Hamilton* of adjustments of couples before marriage he found that the number of men and women who petted to the verge of intercourse and stopped was small compared with those who avoided both petting and intercourse, or with those who went the whole way. This means that if one wishes to avoid intercourse, one should certainly avoid intimate petting. Many young men assume that it will be possible to exert control when they desire but they are likely to find their control has failed when they need it most.

Repeatedly one finds the following behavior pattern. A young man and young woman have a date and spend the evening together. They fall into intimate physical contacts and caresses. Both find themselves sexually stimulated. On succeeding evenings the experience is repeated and the intensity of stimulation mounts. Soon it is easy and natural to take the next step—intercourse. Sex desires, once excited, serve as strong forces to motivate conduct, and rational control becomes difficult. Sometimes the transition from petting to intercourse takes place during a single instance of strong excitation. In these cases there are apt to be no precautions to prevent conception. The experience of Herman, page 98, illustrates a situation of this kind.

The most intimate form of heterosexual adjustment is, of course, sexual intercourse. What proportion of young men indulge in pre-marital relations is much debated and there is no particular value in discussing the question. Experience with young men has led the writer

* Hamilton, G. V., and Macgowan, Kenneth. *What Is Wrong with Marriage?* New York City: Boni. 1929. Page 271.

to believe that promiscuity is not so prevalent as is sometimes indicated. A number of individuals do engage in pre-marital sexual intercourse, but the impression that such relations abound is heightened by the descriptions certain young men give of their exploits. Such descriptions are encouraged by the attitude of the groups that emphasize the desirability and prevalence of this kind of behavior.

Pre-marital intercourse has a varying effect on the individuals who experience it. With some, the relationship has raised further desires and urges and has led to further intercourse. The developmental histories of a number of young men indicate that in a many instances pre-marital relationships, once begun, continue with an increasing degree of frequency and promiscuity. With others the experience was disillusioning, chiefly because conversations had built an expectation not to be realized in actual participation. Still others found the experience disgusting and upsetting, probably as a result of previous moral concepts. Others found that the desire for intercourse, once satisfied, subsided and no longer served as stimulation. The reaction cannot be predicted. To advise a young man to have sexual intercourse to satisfy an occasional physical urge or mental desire is unwise. Other adjustments can be made with much more certainty of good results.

A further danger arising from pre-marital intercourse is conception. Even though many young men use contraceptive devices regularly, a large number of them have inadequate knowledge of how to prevent conception. In very few of the cases that have come under my observation did the individuals using intercourse as a form of adjustment report that they had secured their contraceptive knowledge from authoritative sources. (The issues involved in the use of intercourse as a form of adjustment will be discussed more fully in the following chapter.)

The reasons why individuals participate in intercourse may be summed up under three general headings. First, to satisfy their physical desires. The drives of a sexual nature, which occur in every individual, are accepted by some as drives which cannot be controlled or denied, and satisfaction is sought through sexual relations. Second, the general attitude of the group with which one is associated may lead to a feeling that such relationships are common and desirable. There is evidence that many individuals seek intercourse because the attitude of their group implies a weakness or deficiency in one who has not had it. Many a young man would find it easier to make an adjustment short of intercourse if he could find pleasant associations in a group which emphasized a different standard. It cannot be repeated too often that one's environment has a great deal to do with the type of adjustment made. A third reason for indulgence is that many persons put themselves in the way of intercourse by petting or permitting intimacies in situations which produce strong excitation. To allow such intimacies and still avoid intercourse is extremely difficult.

The ability to control the sexual desires depends upon the attitude of mind which one develops rather than upon the strength of the physical drive. An attitude which is free from morbid interest and leaves no openings for constant stimulation is the key to self control.

[86]

Chapter IV

THE DESIRABILITY OF VARIOUS FORMS
OF ADJUSTMENTS

A SIMPLE DESCRIPTION of the kinds of sex adjustments found in a group of young men above the average in character, social adaptation, and scholastic ability is not enough. The logical "next step" is a discussion of the problems which arise when one form of adjustment or another is used. Most young men want to know what forms are best. A large majority of those with whom I have talked wished more information on the various forms of heterosexual adjustment, especially intercourse. This whole question is so important that it seems necessary to devote an entire chapter to a discussion of the various adjustments, with special emphasis upon the issues involved in sexual intercourse.

It is not my purpose to offer arbitrary or formalized solutions, but to clarify the situation so that clear-thinking young men can make their own decisions. The trouble with dictated formulas is that they must of necessity apply to a given set of circumstances. If, at a later date, the circumstances are different, as is often the case, the formula will not serve. Sex morality is not achieved by manufacturing answers and handing them out. Youth does not readily accept patterns of conduct imposed upon them by their elders. The best way to

[87]

insure moral and socially desirable conduct is to make a clear statement of the issues involved and permit youth to make its own appraisal.

A desirable social adjustment to sex includes much more than a narrow consideration of the physical and anatomical aspects of the question. The general attitude which one holds toward life, one's acceptance of certain ideals and disregard for others—in short one's philosophy of living will markedly effect one's attitude toward sex.

Decisions on sex adjustments are made in relation to a set of values. If these values take other persons into account and emphasize the importance of so living that one's acts bring the maximum satisfaction over an extended period of time both to the individual and his associates, decisions will be different from those of one whose values emphasize only the immediate and physically pleasurable satisfactions. The individual who constantly disregards the rights of others and takes little or no thought of their welfare if it conflicts with his immediate desires, is not likely to be moved by such evidence as may be offered here in support of continence before marriage. To recognize, however, that one's sexual conduct is simply a part of one's whole adjustment to life, and a reflection of the values one holds is the first step in beginning a rational and consciously developed form of adjustment and behavior. The following questions are typical of those most frequently asked by young men: "Is sexual intercourse necessary to health?" "Don't I need experience in sexual relations to make a successful adjustment in marriage?" "Isn't it harmful to suppress sex desires?" "Can I control my sex desires?" "If conception does not result where is the harm?" There are too few such questions as: "What effect may my efforts to secure intercourse have upon the other person?" "May undesirable social consequences follow relationships outside marriage?" "What may be the future effects of this adjustment?" "Who may be effected by this particular kind of conduct other than myself?" Sex desires are sometimes so strong that one seems to forget that there are social effects to be considered.

Shall one perform a dangerous experiment? The answer will differ as one considers performing it in a laboratory with only oneself present, then considers performing it at a party with a roomful of guests. Similarly the answer to the proper sex adjustment may be quite different according to whether one considers one's self only, or one's self in relation to others.

Whether one recognizes it or not, decisions concerning sex adjustment affect others. Even when fanatical sublimation is adopted, with seclusion from worldly contacts, others are affected since they are deprived of associations with a human being. In a complex and interrelated society every decision has its social consequences.

FACTORS INVOLVED IN CONSIDERING ADJUSTMENTS

The desirability of a particular adjustment must be considered from at least four viewpoints.

First, that of the individual himself. Too often he thinks of sex as wholly biological. Equally one-sided is the idea that it is entirely psychological. Analogies are

[89]

dangerous, and to liken sex adjustments to the physical adjustments necessary in the field of exercise, sleep, or diet is to lose sight of the fact that sex adjustments transcend the physical. Psychological, sociological, ethical, and economic factors all require consideration if the best all-round adjustment is to be achieved.

Second, the long-time effects of sex adjustments are very important. So often young men seem to feel that if in pre-marital intercourse, for example, conception does not occur there can be no after effects. Nor does the possibility of earlier adjustments influencing their later behavior or their concepts of sex and family life during middle age occur to them, since they have little realization of the lasting influence of forms of adjustment. The examination of various case studies in this book (for example, that of Anton, on page 91) shows that the effects of adjustment often persist for a long time.

Third, if the adjustment is heterosexual, both partners must be considered. Too often consent on the part of the girl is felt to be sufficient assurance that there will be no harmful results but candid thought will call attention to the effects of such an adjustment upon her as well as upon others directly concerned.

Fourth, the general social welfare should be considered. Unexpected consequences almost inevitably result from wide-spread use of pre-marital intercourse as a form of adjustment. With contemporary society as complex and closely interwoven as it is, the unsocial sex behavior of one person cannot fail to affect others. Therefore the influence upon society as well as upon the individual merits careful thought.

[90]

If incorrect decisions are made and untoward events follow, a number of people secondarily interested are sure to be concerned. The members of one's family, one's friends and associates, even one's acquaintances, will inevitably be affected by sex adjustments which are harmful to the individuals participating. Every youth should stop to consider this. Parents, brothers and sisters, friends, business associates and others, are often vitally affected by the sex adjustments followed by the individual. The following case is an excellent illustration of the results which may come from pre-marital intercourse.

> Anton—Age 20. College sophomore. Very capable intellectually. Held positions of leadership in high school and college. Member of high school honor organization. Well liked in community. Member of highly respected family.
>
> While a senior in high school Anton met and fell in love with Mary, a girl from one of the town's best families. After graduation both enrolled in the small local college. Anton took a pre-law course, while Mary majored in home economics. During their freshman year they took up sexual relationships, largely due to Anton's urgings. Mary felt it might lead to difficulty, but finally agreed. Contraceptive devices were used, but during their sophomore year they realized Mary was pregnant. Then came a period of two months' agonized consideration of courses of action. Marriage was out of the question if Anton was to continue his legal career. Mary was bitter because she felt her predicament was the result of his importunities. Finally they decided to try an abortion. This turned out

badly, and it was with difficulty that Mary's life was saved.

After this, the affair became the common knowledge not only of the immediate families, but of others in the city. Anton and Mary were forced to withdraw from college. Their families, which had been on friendly terms for years, were estranged. The parents of both young people tried to be considerate, but felt that the episode had disgraced them. The publicity attending the incident was unfavorable, and Anton and Mary felt themselves socially ostracized. Mary's mother was so humiliated that she dropped her church and club connections in the city. Whether she will later resume them is a question.

Not only were the parents humiliated, they were grieved over the shattered careers of their children. Anton and Mary severed their relationship as a result of the difficulty. Mary felt that Anton had been very much at fault and very selfish in the whole matter. The incident was so costly that Anton found it impossible to continue his college work elsewhere, and went to a city several hundred miles distant where he secured employment as a grocery clerk. His college career is probably ended as his family, though willing, is unable to help him, and employment conditions are such that he can scarcely hope to save enough for his cherished professional career. He will probably go through life disappointed with respect to his work. When he does marry and have a family they will probably have to accommodate themselves to a standard of living much lower than that to which he has been accustomed, and which he might have provided with a better education.

Mary has also left the city. Her health has not been fully recovered and she has been told by her physician that as a result of her abortion she can never bear children. Her present attitude is one of much bitterness, as she feels that she has been deprived of her cherished hopes. While she refuses to talk about her past experiences she has expressed to her family her intention of never marrying. She has secured work as a telephone operator and is living on a different standard from that to which she has been accustomed. She has practically withdrawn from social contacts and is building a brooding, melancholy nature.

Outside the family there are many other persons adversely affected. Upon Anton's graduation from high school the principal recommended him to the president of the college as a worthy, promising young man and secured for him a substantial scholarship, one of a limited number, at the college. As a result of Anton's difficulty the principal, though sympathetic and understanding, feels that he has been "let down." Further, he finds himself at a disadvantage in further recommendations, as his evaluations tend to be discounted because of his mistake on Anton. Therefore he is unable to give as much help as he would like to other boys applying at the college. It might be noted incidentally, that when Anton received the scholarship it meant that it was denied to some other applicant. The college president is resentful because the unfavorable publicity at the time of the exposure of Anton's and Mary's relationship led to charges that immorality was rife in the student body. The college has felt the effects in the decision of some parents and young people to select a different institution.

[93]

At the beginning of Anton's college work his older brother agreed to give him the financial aid needed to supplement the scholarship. At considerable sacrifice to himself and his family the brother loaned him approximately $450 during the two years. Now the brother is disillusioned and disappointed with Anton and finds that the possibility of Anton's repaying the badly-needed money is remote indeed. As a result the relationship between Anton and his brother and family is severely strained. A younger brother, just graduating from high school, has had to bear the stigma of Anton's conduct. He feels that he has been regarded by parents and young people with suspicion, and to a degree he has been ostracized. Because of this he and his parents thought it best that his college work be taken at some place other than the local college. This can be done only by careful management and sacrifice on the part of himself and his family. At the same time the increased expenditure endangers the chance of a still younger sister to get an education.

The minister of the church which Anton attended has been particularly disturbed. He remarked that Anton's failure to live up to the expectations of his earlier career had come as near as any incident he had ever experienced to destroying his faith in the integrity of young people. Similarly a number of other close friends and neighbors of Anton and his family have been disappointed and grieved over the unfortunate occurrence.

While the situation of Mary and her family and friends is not well enough known to trace a similar chain of effects, it doubtless exists. The better financial condition of Mary's family may have helped somewhat, but the emotional problems remain.

Many young men protest against the operation of community customs in cases of this kind on the grounds that the social attitudes are unsound. Sexual customs and ethics change slowly. One may disagree with existing standards, and yet be obliged to live in a monogamous society in which marked alterations in sexual conduct are unlikely to take place without incurring strong disapproval. Most young men desire to, and eventually will, marry and rear families. If they are to be happy and satisfied, their sexual adjustments before marriage must be in harmony with these ambitions. This means that a monogamous social adjustment and the positive, constructive contributions of sex to happy living need to be kept in mind in determining the most desirable form of pre-marital sexual practice.

A CONSIDERATION OF PETTING

The problems arising from adjustment by pre-marital heterosexual contacts have many aspects other than those already discussed.

Questions are often raised concerning the advisability of petting as a sexual outlet. Petting must be distinguished from other physical contacts which come when two persons are close friends. Physical intimacies growing out of friendly associations are not only inevitable, but desirable if conducted so that passionate desires are not aroused. Two features may be used to differentiate these contacts from petting. Since there is no sharp line of demarcation between them, they must be judged by qualitative, rather than quantitative standards.

First, there is the time element. An embrace, a mutual caress, or good-night kiss as an expression of affection usually lasts but a few seconds at longest. When any of these is drawn out, as when the embrace becomes a matter of lying in each other's arms for extended periods, the contact becomes petting. A normal expression of mutual affection and admiration should not be discouraged. It is undue prolongation of this experience which produces sexual stimulation.

The second feature is the attitude which the participants hold toward their physical relationships. The young man or woman may regard every expression of a physical nature as having a sexual implication. Such a concept places even the simplest physical relationship on a petting basis. Here, obviously, the need is for a broader understanding of what is involved in relationships between men and women. The case of Felix illustrates the difficulty.

> Felix—Age 22. High school graduate. Average student. Particularly interested in the welfare of others, being associated with several charitable activities. Well liked in school and community. Character excellent.
>
> Felix's early environment provided a very unwholesome introduction to sex. He was thrown with a group of older boys and men, all factory workers, whose whole concept of boy-girl relationships was that they existed for sexual satisfactions alone. Every young man was urged to seize any possible opportunity for intercourse. Any young man who escorted a girl to any function was presumed to be doing so in order to secure sexual relations and every item of behavior was interpreted in that light.
>
> Felix's first date on which he took a girl to a movie

[96]

will always remain in his memory. As they walked down the street he was sure it was obvious to everyone that he was experiencing an erection. He was too bashful to pet, but several times in the theater when his hand touched that of the girl, or their shoulders brushed, he responded with a strong erection. The same thing occurred when he bade her good-night. Succeeding dates brought similar experiences.

Later Felix came to know very well a young man who served as his scoutmaster. The young man gave him careful instruction in sex and Felix found it possible to talk with him fully and easily. The result was a marked alteration in his sexual concepts. Within a year or so he noted that quite close physical contacts of short duration, had no effect in producing a sexual stimulation.

As previously indicated, petting in this discussion refers to the use of intimate physical associations to induce sex excitation and stimulation. So defined it is a way of securing sexual gratification, and its practice is certain to make it more difficult to refrain from intercourse. The couple may desire to secure only a certain amount of physical stimulation; their intention is usually to stop short of intercourse. On the other hand, some young men use petting as an exploratory and exciting device intended to lead to sexual relations. In such cases there is, of course, no intent to exercise self-control. Petting may be used by both boys and girls for a variety of other purposes as well. They may desire to see how the other person will react, or they may wish to get revenge on an absent lover. There are many other motives, simple or complex, and there are many cases of petting which are simply drifted into without conscious intent.

Dr. Paul Popenoe* has described petting as a "starvation phenomenon." This grows out of the fact that it is often the result of a lack of normal, wholesome social activities involving members of both sexes. Individuals who have enjoyed the company of girls, then find themselves unable to avail themselves of such company, sometimes react by indulgence in petting. For an example, see the case history of Philip on page 184, Chapter VII. Frequent associations with girls under circumstances where interesting activities take place and pleasant personalities enliven friendship are far more likely to develop a desirable attitude toward physical contacts than a prolonged absence of such associations.

Three dangers are involved in stimulating the sexual desires through petting. First, if a young man really wishes to avoid intercourse, this is a poor way to begin. Petting, certainly "heavy petting," is a natural preliminary to sexual intercourse. The process may be repeated a number of times and each time stop short of intercourse, but this is playing with fire. Constant stirring of the emotions is likely to raise them to a point where control becomes difficult, if not impossible. To this many young men can testify. The case of Herman is one of many.

> Herman—Age 20. College student. Average in scholarship. Some participation in athletics. Average social adjustment.

* Dr. Popenoe is Director of the Institute of Family Relations, Los Angeles, California.

Herman had been reared in a strictly religious home where high standards of morality were stressed. He had had no actual sex instruction. He made some use of petting as a method of getting sexual satisfaction, the intent being to stop short of intercourse. When about twenty, Herman began a petting episode with a girl who, plainly desiring intercourse, intentionally tried to arouse stronger passions. He either could not or did not exercise control and intercourse occurred. His conclusion was that the exercise of control depended much upon the partner.

Little safety lies in the belief that one will never go too far. The references to Hamilton and Macgowan,* cited in a previous chapter, showed that the number who did not indulge in petting or intercourse before marriage, and those who indulged in both were much larger than the number who indulged in petting but not intercourse. There seemed to be almost no middle ground. Bluntly and squarely, the situation may be put thus: The experience of others shows that if you don't want to go the whole way, you had better not start.

Those who find it possible to stop face still another problem—that of fastening their adjustment on this level of physical gratification. This point should not be emphasized beyond its importance, yet in my experience in counseling with young men, I have found several instances (two of which are cited below) which indicate that the danger of such an adjustment may exist.

* Hamilton, G. V., and Macgowan, Kenneth, *What Is Wrong with Marriage?* New York City: Boni. 1929. Page 271.

Nathan—Age 19. College junior. Intellectually above the average, though scholastic standing is only average. Participates widely in extracurricular activities. Social adjustment in certain groups excellent, in others, average.

Since the age of sixteen, Nathan has secured a great deal of sexual stimulation from petting. He has participated in prolonged petting episodes with different girls once or twice weekly. The physical intimacies produce marked sexual stimulation, but the experience has never been carried beyond the petting level. At first he found this unsatisfactory, as it seemed to leave him in need of a further outlet. Usually he resorted to masturbation. Later he found that the difficulty of stopping at the point of strong stimulation was not so great, and the experience was more satisfying. He himself believes that there has been an increasing tendency to fix upon petting as a form of sexual adjustment.

Oran—Age 24. College graduate. Intellectual capacity and scholastic standing above average. Holds position of leadership with boys. Very active participant in athletics.

Oran took up petting as a form of adjustment, supplementing masturbation which he had begun about five years before, at sixteen. He had contacts with a number of girls during the next four years, all on this level. About four years ago he took up this adjustment exclusively with one girl. Since then he has indulged in petting episodes about three times a month, each time to the point of ejaculation. With him this is a method of satisfying sexual desires. He has debated a number of times about the desirability of intercourse

[100]

but it has never seemed right. The physical and mental desire for relations, according to Oran, is, however, very definite.

Oran believes that for him sexual gratification has not been fixed on petting. He feels certain that if married he could take up sexual intercourse and experience the usual satisfaction. This belief seems open to question, particularly since he has been using this form of adjustment for about eight years. And even if this belief is correct for him, it does not answer the question for his partner, or for others following the same practice. There is a possibility that, as a result of such extensive experience on this level, normal intercourse will be less satisfying for him, and in turn for his wife, than it should be.

Intimate physical associations between a man and woman who care much for each other are likely to lead to problems of control. If difficulties are to be avoided, both must recognize the problem and coöperate in so ordering their conduct as to make adjustment easier. The need for this is illustrated in the case of Arthur, a twenty-four-year-old college graduate, and an honor student, whose earlier history is described on page 49.

Arthur and his fiancée were faced with the problem of making an adjustment to the sexual desires growing out of intense love. They agreed that they preferred to avoid intercourse, basing their association on other interests instead. Music, art, and books as well as a common college curriculum gave them plenty of opportunity to work together at interesting activities. Hiking occupied a part of their leisure time. Vexing, complex problems were thus avoided, and intercourse never occurred. Both found this adjustment satisfactory.

At least two requisites were involved. The first was the existence of other interests besides sex. One reason so many young people find their interests almost inevitably turning toward sex is that they have little else in common. The second requisite was the determination of Arthur and his fiancée not to subject themselves voluntarily to situations in which they would be unduly stimulated or where sex urges would over-shadow all else. There was, for example, no heavy petting in dark, out-of-the-way corners.

The third danger is the effect heavy petting may have upon the girl. The boy may come out of the experience unscathed but this is no assurance that the girl will emerge from it equally free. Mere willingness to enter the relationship does not mean that undesirable results will not follow, despite the fact that some so argue. Willingness may be the result of previous undesirable sexual experiences. The girl may also feel that the only way to avoid being a wallflower is to submit to such intimacies. Whatever the reason, she may well suffer unfortunate consequences. There is as much danger for her as for her partner that sexual satisfaction will be fixed on this level. Or, again, the practice may arouse desires which she will find difficult to control. Still another possibility is that the stimulation of emotions which occurs in petting will create a feeling of attachment which neither party is in a position to encourage. Such a situation is described in the case of Joseph.

Joseph—Age 24. University senior. Above average student. Active in sports, captain of basketball team. President of class and fraternity. Respected and well liked by both older and younger people.

During the summer following Joseph's freshman year in college he served as a waiter in a restaurant in one of the national parks. Here he became acquainted with a college girl of his own age, a waitress in the same restaurant. They spent many evenings together. The relationship was kept on a friendly basis until near the close of the summer when one evening they drifted into a "heavy petting" episode. Joseph found the experience decidedly stimulating and took occasion to repeat it every night during the remainder of their three weeks in the park. He really cared for the girl only as a friend and never permitted their intimacies to go further than intensive petting.

At the end of the three weeks, Joseph was chagrined to find that the girl had fallen deeply in love with him. She showed great emotional disturbance at parting, and after he returned to the university, wrote several pleading letters which he did not answer. Later the overwrought girl called him by telephone and he told her the "stuff just had to be off, no two ways about it." This seems to have closed the incident, since he has heard nothing further from her. He feels himself to blame and says he is very much depressed about the whole affair.

INTERCOURSE AS A FORM OF PRE-MARITAL ADJUSTMENT

The proper attitude to take toward intercourse is a question which confronts practically every physically normal young man. The sexually stimulating influences in the modern world, the extraordinary ease of making contacts with many people and many environments, along with greater freedom in the social attitude toward sex, make it almost inevitable that the question shall arise.

Intercourse as an adjustment may occur in relationships involving various degrees of acquaintanceship. In the first place, it may result from brief or transitory contacts. Girls picked up from the streets, in public dance halls, at theatres, or in similar places provide opportunities for such intimacy. Recourse to public prostitutes is also included on this level.

Such relationships are definitely injudicious and undesirable, and those who take part in them do so without regard for anything beyond the immediate physical satisfaction of their own desires. It is significant that they ignore the possible social effects of their conduct and that they fail to take into account the influence it may have on their later adjustments in marriage. Psychologically, promiscuous behavior indicates an attitude which is likely to hamper later adjustments. Gilbert and Emmett, whose histories are given below, illustrate the serious change that promiscuous relations can cause in one's point of view.

Gilbert—Age 26. Graduated from college with high honors. Able public speaker. Well liked by associates. Member of two scholarship fraternities and a social fraternity.

Gilbert had his first experience at coitus sometime between the ages of nine and eleven. No further experience occurred until sixteen when sexual relations were taken up regularly. Over a period of ten years he has had intercourse on the average of two or three times weekly. During this time he has had affairs with approximately fifteen girls. Practically all the relationships have been based upon the desire for physical pleasure and gratification.

Gilbert expressed doubts that he could now fall in love in the normal way. He felt that promiscuity had caused him to appraise all women from the sexual point of view and regretted that this aspect of sex had come to assume a place of so much importance in his thinking.

Emmett—Age 24. College student. Average mental ability. Scholastic record average. Some participation in athletics. Holds some positions of leadership. Quite interested in social affairs. A regular attendant at dances and similar activities.

Emmett was reared in an environment where there was little supervision. His parents died while he was young and he lived with his grandparents. Much of his time was spent on the streets where he learned about sex in the usual lascivious way. The attitude with which he was familiar and which he held was that sex was to be played with for the gratification of sensual desires.

At an early age Emmett met a girl with whom he soon succeeded in having intercourse. No other instances occurred until age twenty-one when he carried on an affair with another girl during a summer vacation. Later, he had intercourse over varying periods of time with two or three other individuals. During one of the later affairs he was keeping company with a girl whom he felt he "really loved." This girl he "wouldn't think of touching." She was not aware of his clandestine sexual intercourse with the other girl, and Emmett, largely because of advice given during an interview, gave it up. Six months later, however, he entered into a similar relationship with another partner. Meantime his love affair had gone on the rocks.

Emmett states that he has come to regard sex largely as a physical matter and girls chiefly as a means of sexual gratification. It will be difficult, he feels, for him to love any girl the way one should if one plans to marry. He regrets his career of promiscuous intercourse.

One cannot be certain about the future, but it seems a fairly safe guess that Emmett has seriously jeopardized his chances of a happy marriage except as he may realize his own danger and consciously guard against it. Usually neither husband nor wife is ready to tolerate sexual promiscuity in the other. The divorce courts alone offer sufficient evidence that such behavior is not conducive to happy marriage. That Emmett did not tell his fiancée he was having intercourse with another person shows that he did not expect her to accept the situation.

Another reason given for entering into chance sexual relationships is the desire many young men feel for experience in intercourse. The individual is eager to know what it is like and to get the elation and satisfaction which he has been led to expect will result from it. Such a desire, once aroused, may be hard to handle wisely. The arousal may have been caused and sustained by environmental influences such as associates, literature, movies, or stimulating incidents. It is important, if this is the case, to alter or eliminate the exciting influences, for the possible effects of intercourse resulting from chance contacts are such that under any circumstances abstinence is better than indulgence.

Young men feeling this marked desire for intercourse are sometimes advised by associates to satisfy it, the assumption being that this will do away with the desire. Considering the effect from a purely individual viewpoint, the best that can be said is that sometimes the desire is eliminated, and that, having once experienced intercourse, the individual forgets his craving. More often such an experience serves to arouse desires of greater intensity.

The difficulty in advising the individual to satisfy his sexual urges through intercourse is that such advice may plunge him, and through him others, into promiscuous relationships. The existence of a strong desire for sexual relations over a period of time, with an opposing feeling that it is better to avoid such relations, is indicative of a conflict which may be intensified by intercourse. If such a conflict had not existed, it is probable either that the desire would have been satisfied earlier or that the longing would not have persisted with such intensity. There is no assurance that experience will solve the difficulty. Desires aroused by the discussions of associates and by conditions in one's environment will continue as long as the conditions which give rise to them remain.

The case of a highly intelligent and socially-minded young man enrolled in the law school of a large university illustrates the possibility of control by a change of association. Since high school days he had felt a desire for sexual intercourse. His associates in the college fraternity stimulated this feeling. For some time he debated the desirability of intercourse, but decided against it. Seeking a method of making his adjustment easier, he decided to change his associates. He therefore moved into a house with a friend whose interests, like his own, were in a field of professional preparation. These circumstances made self-control much simpler. The desire did not disappear, but was so much less pronounced that it caused him little further concern.

Still another aid comes from talking over the whole problem frankly and objectively with someone—if a suitable person can be found. The very mystery that beclouds sex serves to stimulate curiosity and longing. A number of young men have discovered that an open discussion of their adjustment with someone who could regard it with detachment has been extremely helpful. From my experience in talking with young men on this problem, I make this point of discussing sexual adjustment openly and objectively as a strong recommendation, recognizing at the same time that advisers who can so discuss the matter are not easy to find. A careful study of good literature in which the subject is treated scientifically is the next best approach.

If individual welfare alone were to be considered, one might more readily condone resort to intercourse for satisfaction of a strong sex urge. This would be assuming that the individual had done what he could to make his environment desirable, and had faced the question directly and squarely. Even then, disregarding all thoughts of possible consequences to others, the wisdom of such advice might be sharply questioned because of extreme uncertainty that the procedure would produce the desired results.

Sexual relations between chance acquaintances carry a high risk of contracting venereal diseases. On page 147 a reference is cited which attributes twenty-five per cent of venereal infection to contacts arising from such relationships. There is no certain method for avoiding these diseases. Prophylactic devices and immediate treatment after intercourse cut down the risk but do not eliminate it. The greatest danger comes in the false sense of security which arises after several experiences from which venereal diseases are not contracted. After successfully evading a disease for some time the individual comes to feel that elaborate precautions are not worth the time and effort. Many feel that cautions apply to the other fellow—not to themselves. The experiences of young men, however, indicate that most of them started with the resolve to exercise adequate care, but soon came to exercise little or none. Such carelessness, especially in promiscuous contacts, may lead to the contraction of a venereal disease.

Sexual intercourse between mutual friends constitutes another form of relationship, but many of the points emphasized above apply here also. Perhaps in several ways adjustment on this level assumes a more serious aspect than adjustment on the level just discussed.

The attitude toward sex resulting when young people engage in such relations freely within their group is likely to result in a complete disregard of the monogamous aspects of marriage. That is, being accustomed to free associations on this level, they keep sex relations entirely divorced from the idea of loyalty or faithfulness to any one person. For some this pattern of thought and conduct readily carries over into marriage, and it does not take an expert in family relationships to know that promiscuity after marriage is in a very high percentage of cases detrimental to happy adjustments within marriage.

Even if an individual escapes these consequences, his actions may result in such bad adjustments on the part of others that their chances for a successful life will be ruined. Such possibilities may bear little or no weight with those who consider only their own interests, but that they exist is clearly indicated by individual experiences, such as that of Anton cited on page 91.

The risk of disease is perhaps not so great in promiscuous relations on the acquaintance level as in chance relationships, but a real danger lies in the probability that some member will go outside the group, contract a disease, and return to infect others before the danger is known. An infection, once started, obviously could and would spread rapidly.

Should conception occur, or knowledge of promiscuous relationships become known outside the group, the effect on those secondarily concerned is likely to be much greater than in chance relationships. Parents and friends are more apt to be affected, and individual careers more readily blighted under these conditions.

No detailed description is required to make clear what might be the effects of such a situation.

The possibility of difficulties from pre-marital intercourse should not be minimized, nor should it be over-emphasized. Unthinkingly people have tried too long to make young people good by frightening them. Having once found that the situation was falsely represented or that a method of controlling dangerous factors had been devised, some young people saw few reasons left for being moral. Frankness presents a more stable foundation for morality than fear, and the dangers of pre-marital intercourse should be dealt with from this standpoint.

Despite the use of various types of commercial devices for preventing conception, there is no method upon which one can rely with certainty. Conception is still a possibility. Writing of commercialized contraceptive devices in the "Consumers Defender" for December, 1935, Dr. Eric M. Matsner, medical director of the American Birth Control League, says, "More than three hundred different firms are manufacturing products for contraception in the United States. . . . Tests have shown that the great majority of these products are inferior and unreliable. Some of them are definitely harmful."

A common practice for avoiding conception is the observance of the so-called safe-period, sometimes called the rhythmic method of contraception. This method is based upon the assumption that there is a certain time in the menstrual cycle when conception will not occur. Nearly all authorities, however, feel that

[111]

this contraceptive practice is conditioned by so many uncontrolled and unobservable factors that dependence upon the "safe-period" is quite an unsafe method of preventing conception. The following quotation* gives a clear statement concerning some of the problems involved. ". . . other factors (other than the relation between the time of the release of the ovum, or egg, and the time of menstruation) play an equally important rôle in the study of periodic fertility. The life span of the human ovum and the length of time necessary for its passage through the fallopian tubes has not been definitely determined and opinion varies as to the average length of time of viability of human spermatozoa after deposition in the female genital tract. Furthermore, calculation of the non-fertile days presupposes relative menstrual regularity, single ovulation, and recorded study of the menstrual history of the individual patient as well as a definite record extending over at least twelve months.

"All of the safe period formulae require a period of abstinence in the mid-menstrual period of the cycle, varying between seven and twelve days, to allow for a range of ovulation and slight menstrual irregularity."

"Latz† states that the safe period should not be recommended:

(a) After confinement, miscarriage, or abortion until

* Matsner, Eric M. *The Techniques of Contraception.* New York: National Medical Council on Birth Control. Pp. 35-36.

† Latz, Leo J. *The Rhythm of Sterility and Fertility in Women.* Chicago: Latz Foundation. 1934.

[112]

a regularity of the cycle is reëstablished. (Usually from three to six months.)

(b) After febrile and debilitating diseases or severe physical injuries.

(c) After severe psychic or emotional upsets.

(d) After any drastic alteration in the ordinary routine of life, such as prolonged travel in a strange climate and strenuous exercise."

Dr. Robert L. Dickinson, a pioneer worker in this field and author of an authoritative book on conception,* states that there is no time in the menstrual cycle in which conception has not occurred in some women.

Further investigational work recently published† indicates still more uncertainty in regard to the use of the safe period as a contraceptive method. One of the tentative and possible conclusions of the research is that the time at which the egg is released may vary considerably from one menstrual cycle to another in the same person, and may be considerably different in different individuals. If this conclusion (which is not definitely proved) be true then conception may occur within wider ranges during the menstrual period than has been supposed.

Concerning the "safe period" method Dr. Matsner writes: "Dr. Knaus (an Austrian authority on this method of birth control) told me that before his method

* Dickinson, Robert L., M.D., and Bryant, Louise Stevens. *Control of Conception.* Baltimore: Williams and Wilkins. 1936.

† Gustavson, R. G., and others. "The Quantitative Determination of Estrogenic Substance in Normal Female Urine During the Menstrual Cycle." *American Journal of Obstetrics and Gynecology.* 35:115-123. January, 1938.

could be put into practice with any degree of reliability there must be a careful observation (and a written record)* of each patient's individual cycle for a period of one year to 18 months." Dr. Matsner also writes of this method, "There is insufficient scientific evidence to prove that the method is applicable to all women."

Still other investigations raise further questions in regard to the effectiveness of observing the "safe period." As a result of evidence growing out of researches the hypothesis has been formed that in some women two ovulations may occur between menstrual periods. Another possibility is that in some cases, under the influence of strong sexual stimulation, an egg may be released for fertilization at the time of sexual intercourse.

Withdrawal before ejaculation is used as a contraceptive method by some couples. Dr. Matsner in his pamphlet "The Technique of Contraception" lists withdrawal as a contraceptive method which is "impractical for general use, uncertain, and questionable."

Dr. Robert L. Dickinson† says: "Withdrawal is only successful with those sufficiently experienced, and its failures range high."

Reliable methods of contraception must be worked out with the advice and help of a competent physician. Even then, uniform success has not been secured, the rate of success given by Dr. Matsner in the above reference ranging from ninety-three to ninety-seven per cent.

If the proportion of success ranges from ninety-three

* Phrase in parentheses inserted in the original quotation by Dr. Matsner in a personal letter to the author, May 4, 1937.
† Personal letter to the author, July 6, 1937. Quoted by permission.

to ninety-seven per cent under the most favorable conditions, one should expect the percentage growing out of the use of contraceptive devices in pre-marital intercourse to be even lower, especially since such intercourse has usually to be carried out, perhaps hastily, under secretive and clandestine conditions which are not at all conducive to the careful use of contraceptive devices.

Abortions* are sometimes used to escape the responsibilities of childbirth and later care of the child. Anyone who knows the truth about abortions, their illegality, their effect upon health, even to the point of endangering life itself, will accept this method as a desirable solution with the greatest hesitancy. An attitude toward abortion often found among those carrying on promiscuous relationships was indicated by the remark of a young man engaging in pre-marital intercourse who said that if conception did occur, it really did not matter since abortions were cheap and easy to obtain. If he had been the person facing the possible effects of an abortion, one wonders whether he would have assumed such nonchalance.

The truth is that abortions levy a terrific toll every year not only in the loss of life among unborn children, but in the death or physical disability of hundreds of women. The whole practice takes on the appearance of a conscienceless traffic when the facts are known. Because abortions are illegal, and the necessity for them often the result of socially and legally disapproved re-

* Abortion is the act of removing or forcing the unborn infant from the body of the mother. This usually occurs early in the period of gestation or pregnancy.

lationships, the facts are shrouded in secrecy. Yet back of this secrecy lies a practice exacting so heavy a social and financial cost that everything possible should be done to discourage it.

Further, the possible long-time effects must be balanced against the immediate desires. Sex satisfaction gained through promiscuous relationships may imperil the success of a career. Reputations are easily ruined and careers cut short if conception should be the result of intercourse. Also; a past history which conceals socially disapproved conduct often proves a liability to one who had started to climb toward success. The story of promiscuous conduct is often started against people in public life by enemies, and if there is a foundation for it there is great danger that one's career will be blasted.

The tendency to narrow the circle from which one can choose a mate is another result of pre-marital intercourse. Many young men and women insist that they will not marry anyone who has had pre-marital experiences. Young men, who make virginity a requisite on the part of their mates, all too often carry on pre-marital relationships themselves. The unfairness of such conduct escapes them or is ignored. A young man may demand the single standard on the part of his prospective marriage partner, and at the same time carry on intercourse with another girl, thus keeping her from meeting the same standard when exacted of her by another man who holds the same ideal. Pre-marital intercourse as prevalently practiced will either limit the number of persons from which one may choose a partner, or necessitate the building of a different standard.

[116]

Continual experience in promiscuous sexual affairs tends to produce a careless attitude in the participants towards both the physical and ethical aspects of the relationship. Every young man who begins pre-marital sex intimacies probably resolves firmly that he will take such precautions that there will be no unwanted pregnancy or venereal disease. With the accumulation of experiences in which he escapes without mishap he is likely to feel that he has mastered the technique for escaping disaster. Then he becomes careless and runs into the trouble that was certain almost from the beginning. The two cases cited below, of Leo and Benjamin, illustrate this point.

Leo—Age 22. Reached sophomore year in college. Able student. Particularly active in social affairs. Well liked and respected.

During Leo's freshman year in college, he and his fiancée had pre-marital sexual relations. They used the common contraceptive devices, and took the common precautions. They desired to avoid pregnancy, for their plan was to wait for marriage until Leo had finished his college work and was ready to enter the professional school.

Early in the sophomore year Leo and his fiancée attended a dance. A petting episode followed and intercourse occurred. It happened that Leo was without contraceptive devices, but they decided to go ahead anyway as the girl stated that the time of the menstrual cycle was such that pregnancy would not occur. Shortly afterwards it was determined that she was pregnant. Early efforts to induce a miscarriage failed, and the parents of the couple were informed of the situation.

They refused to sanction an abortion. Thereupon Leo and his fiancée withdrew from college and were married. Leo found it necessary to sacrifice his professional career, accepting a position as time-keeper on a construction job.

Benjamin—Age 23. College sophomore. Member of football team. Below average student. Average in social attributes.

Benjamin told of carrying on a pre-marital sex affair with a girl, long an acquaintance of his family. The association had been going on for about six months with intercourse occurring once or twice a week. For the first four months the couple had practiced withdrawal as a means of preventing conception. This had proved unsatisfactory to both. The new adjustment was to carry out intercourse as before, and to have the girl follow such procedures for contraception as she deemed best after she had returned home.

Both seemed unaware that in this period of time it was entirely possible for some of the sperm cells, or spermatozoa, to have reached the ovum, in which case conception might already have occurred.

Another aspect of this laxity occurs in the disregard which some individuals show in the welfare of their partner. They take the position that "she is of age, and can look out for herself." Such persons take only the precautions which seem needed to insure their own safety. The case of Ivan typifies this point of view.

Ivan—Age 23. College graduate. Above average in mental ability. Active participant in athletics. Social adjustment good. Has held some positions of leadership. Well liked by associates.

Before coming to college Ivan had had sexual experiences a number of times with each of nine girls. All nine had been friends or acquaintances for several years. Contraceptives were used, and all precautions taken to avoid difficulty.

Between his sophomore and junior year in college he traveled quite widely in a remote section of the United States. He stopped a number of times at places where he could find labor, and worked for a few days to several weeks. In six of these brief stops he engaged in sexual intimacies with girls. With no one of the six did he use any contraceptive safeguard. He told the girls he would withdraw before ejaculation, but actually did not. He recognized that his deception had made each girl bear the whole responsibility for the affair. His comment was, "I knew we would never see each other again, and I hadn't given my correct name or address, so I just didn't seem to care."

Most important of all is the effect promiscuous premarital intercourse often has in altering one's attitude toward the entire concept of sex and its place in living. Properly conceived and properly handled, sex can become a positive, constructive force tempering the whole of life. Sanely used, it can become an integral part of a full and rich love relationship; unwholesomely used it turns love to ashes and hope to despair. It can contribute to a happy, satisfying family life if properly directed; if improperly directed, it can destroy all hopes of ever building such happiness. The problem of securing correct attitudes toward sex and developing proper adjustments would be much easier if young people could understand how much sex can contribute to happy successful living. They need also to realize that this contribution is endangered, if not destroyed, by promiscuous relationships, lustful desires, and lascivious attitudes.

A rather prevalent social attitude, passing as liberal, tends to discount the constructive emphasis made in the preceding paragraph. These so-called liberals feel that references to sex as a constructive factor which needs to be exercised within the bounds of social convention are moralistic and more concerned with abstract ethics than everyday living. Unfortunately, in too many discussions, the moral and ethical aspects of sex behavior are neglected; or if discussed, they are supported chiefly by emotional appeals rather than by demonstrable facts showing undesirable social and individual consequences.

Any psychologist or sociologist can point to many ill effects arising from the failure to use sex constructively. The psychologist sees the generation of unwholesome attitudes, complexes and obsessions because the individual has misused sex and misconceived its function. The sociologist sees the social cost of illegitimacy, venereal disease, the unhappy and broken homes and the maladjusted children coming from them. These results are obvious to anyone who has studied the issues carefully.

The social effects of promiscuous intercourse or premarital relations between engaged couples have yet to be considered. Ordinarily it is difficult to get people, young or old, to weigh long-time social effects. There are several reasons for this. One is that such effects are intangible—it is difficult to point to a specific condition and prove that it is the certain result of a given course of action. Again, such results usually are not confined to the individual. In few cases do the long-time social effects fall directly and completely upon a single person. Rather they tend to be diffused through the entire population. Finally, the results are too remote in time to cause much concern. The immediate consequences are more pressing and seemingly more important. One of the marked needs of our society is the willingness to consider the solution of problems from a social point of view. A short-time, individualistic solution often operates directly against the ultimate welfare.

Family instability is one of the chief social evils arising from pre-marital intercourse of a promiscuous or semi-promiscuous nature. Young people whose pattern of sex conduct has largely or entirely ignored the monogamous standard are likely to find it difficult to adjust themselves to constancy in the marriage relationship, where neither partner is likely to accept promiscuity in the other. Broken homes and dissolved marriages are many times the outgrowth of improper patterns of sex conduct before marriage. Pre-marital sexual experiences do not inevitably result in adultery, and such a conclusion is not to be drawn from this statement, but promiscuous behavior before marriage induces a readiness to seek a variety of sexual experiences after the vows of fidelity have been taken.

Three scientific studies have been attempted to show

to what extent this is true. Katharine B. Davis* made a study of women who were happily and unhappily married. Of the group who were unhappy, fifteen and two-tenths per cent had had intercourse before marriage, while of the happily married group but two and five-tenths per cent had experienced intercourse.

Hamilton and Macgowan† also discuss this issue in the report of their interesting investigations. Of the men and women who had not experienced intercourse before marriage, they found that fifty-seven per cent of the men and forty-nine per cent of the women were happily married. Of those who had had intercourse before marriage, only forty-six per cent of the men and thirty-seven per cent of the women were happily married. Those who had committed adultery were distinctly less happy than the rest.

The report summed up the matter as follows: "Finally what relationship can be traced between virginity and adultery—for men and for women? Certainly the non-virgins were more adulterous than the virgins. But sexual experiences before the wedding night did not drive the women on to any unusual restlessness in marriage compared with the men. The experienced men continued to be more adulterous, and their faithlessness increased more than the women's. Which is pretty much the general picture you might have expected. . . . The old theory that a young fellow should sow his wild oats in order to marry successfully and remain faithful in

* Davis, Katharine B. *Factors in the Sex Life of Twenty-two Hundred Women.* New York City: Harper and Brothers. 1929.
† Hamilton, Gilbert V., and Macgowan, Kenneth. *What Is Wrong with Marriage?* New York: Boni. 1929. Page 234ff.

marriage is about as common as a newer theory that pre-marital experience is liable to set up a habit of promiscuity. The truth is probably a more mixed and temperate statement."

Terman devised a way to determine whether those who had no intercourse before marriage were happier in marriage than those who had experienced such relations. He concludes that* "in general those husbands and wives who were either virgins at marriage or had had intercourse only with each other tend to have higher mean happiness scores than the other groups. . . . Pre-marital strictness in regard to sex may or may not be the *cause* of the greater happiness. It may, instead, merely tend to select the persons who by ideals and personality have greater natural aptitude for successful marital adjustment, while laxness before marriage may tend to select those with less of this aptitude. Whichever interpretation is correct, the practical implications are the same, other things being equal, one's chances of marital happiness are at present favored by the selection of a mate who has not had intercourse with any other person."

Dr. Paul Popenoe points to still another possible outcome of pre-marital relations. His experience in counseling with people having domestic difficulty indicates that pre-marital intercourse may lead the partners to suspect each other of infidelity after marriage. Particularly is this true if there is some incident or behavior which may create suspicion. The husband, for

* Terman, Lewis M. *Psychological Factors in Marital Happiness.* New York: McGraw Hill Book Co., Inc. 1938. Page 329.

example, may think, "Well, my wife shared such relations with me. If she was willing to accept such attentions from me before marriage, how can I be sure she will not accept similar attentions after marriage?" And so the scene is set for strife and discord. Evidence does not lend support to the theory that experimentation in sex is essential for or conducive to a happy marriage.

Still more important is the problem resulting from the attempt to rear children in these socially inadequate homes. A child brought up in a family in which the parents are in conflict is almost certain to be poorly adjusted. A divided home cannot produce an integrated individual. The experience of a few years of psychological counseling would do much to convince young people of the importance of this. A counselor who comes to grips with the maladjustments of children and adolescents spends many a futile hour trying to correct conditions which many times are almost entirely the reflection of parental difficulties. The case of Garnett on pages 179 to 182 illustrates this.

Such difficulties in many cases, are the result of undesirable adjustments occurring before the birth of the child. Not all family difficulties and domestic discord are basically sexual, although sexual incompatibility does give rise to trouble. A knowledge of the important influence of good family environment upon the rearing of children makes clear the necessity for eliminating as far as possible all factors tending to maladjustment.

A third social outcome of freedom in sexual relations is that such behavior sets a precedent for others. If one person demands the right to freedom or promiscuity, others will demand it. Without doubt there are no immediate ill effects from many pre-marital affairs, but in other cases venereal disease, abortions, children born out of wedlock, and hasty and ill-advised marriages result.

Young people pay a tremendous individual and social price for their freedom to experiment with sex. This cost is totaled not only in dollars and cents, but also in blighted lives, wrecked health, careers cut short, broken homes, and disorganized families. To establish a standard of continence before marriage would be an important step in improving conditions. The elimination of promiscuous and pre-marital sexual relations, it must be recognized, would not wipe out all the social evils enumerated but such relations must bear a heavy part of the responsibility for them.

Unfortunately many young people are unable to foresee the consequences clearly enough to realize what is involved. These consequences may persist for years. To foresee them, or to observe them at a later period, and relate them to earlier behavior is difficult if not impossible. Persons involved in misfortunes as a result of previous inadequate sex adjustments are often reluctant to admit it. Instead they are likely to meet the situation with bravado or rationalization. Unable, as an observer from the outside, to see the cause and effect relationship, the inexperienced person is not likely to conclude that promiscuous sexual conduct is responsible.

The case of Maurice illustrates in a concrete way the

results of promiscuity. Even in this instance, the effects are far from being terminated.

Maurice—Age 25. College graduate. Able intellectually. Academic standing average. Social adjustment to groups fair.

Maurice was, from early childhood, brought into contact with sex in a way that constantly stimulated desires and passions. He lived in an industrial community and his early activities were unsupervised. He was associated with a group of young men who constantly jested about sex and used it as a means of sensual gratification. He was introduced to sex practices when very young, being induced to try intercourse at about eight years of age. Further, the gang with which he associated used to masturbate in groups and Maurice began the practice himself before sex maturity. Masturbation was regarded as an evidence of vitality and prowess, and the strongest individual was the one who could masturbate most frequently.

Lacking close supervision at home, Maurice took up intercourse as a continuous form of adjustment when about fifteen. He and a close companion abandoned themselves to a search for sensual pleasure. They were quite promiscuous, and over the period of eight years, from age fifteen to twenty-three, Maurice estimated that he had intercourse with fifty or sixty different persons. With a few of his mistresses he has had relationships continuously over a period of time, others he has met but a few times, and still others were chance acquaintances.

Maurice discussed the effects of his experiences objectively and at length. He could note no physical ill-effects from either masturbation or intercourse. He did feel definitely, however, that there were other effects. He remarked that he knew that he had come to appraise every girl from the physical viewpoint. He paid little or no attention to cultural or intellectual attainments and observed that if he ever married it would be to have someone who could keep house for him. Sexually, he is satisfied that he could never tie himself down to one woman all the rest of his life. He feels also that no two persons married nowadays, intend to remain faithful to each other. There is, according to Maurice, little fidelity in the marriage relationship and "stepping out" is common and expected. Despite this expressed cynicism, Maurice did not leave the impression of being a cynic.

Maurice's chief regret was that his pursuit of sensual delight had left him unsatisfied. He was unable to express his dissatisfaction clearly, but "something seemed to be lacking." He seemed to have nothing to tie to, and was going ahead without aim or direction. The whole tenor of his discussion left one feeling that when he permitted himself to face his situation frankly, he found himself a very unhappy young man.

When questioned about the social effects of his adjustment, he remarked that one thing he prided himself on was his care in protecting himself. He felt that he was "much more careful than the usual fellow." He had never had a venereal disease, though in a couple of instances he had had examinations to check his condition.

When asked about the effect of his promiscuity on others, Maurice said that he had some things to regret. In one instance he had caused a girl to become pregnant and a miscarriage had followed. In another the girl had tried to escape the consequences by an abortion. Maurice was sorry these instances had occurred, and said that they were "mishaps resulting from pure carelessness."

Maurice had several affairs with married women. He stated that he did not feel he had been instrumental in causing difficulties for them. They were already dissatisfied with their marital state or they would never have been willing to have intercourse with him.

Maurice also said that in several instances he had broken off an affair because the girl had fallen too deeply in love with him and he could not reciprocate the feeling. Several of these girls, he knew, had had a difficult time in making satisfactory readjustment.

At the time of the interview, Maurice was having sexual relations on the average of once or twice weekly. He had also in the last year been drinking rather heavily. He felt in a way that this was foolish, but it represented a release for him. He was just at that time graduating from college and in search of work. He was, however, having no success because, he felt, people knew him too well, and the college placement bureau was not standing behind him. Maurice was not condemnatory for he felt that knowing his reputation they could not support him. The situation was discouraging and his despondency found its outlet in drinking.

A study of the case history of Maurice and others may have raised a question as to whether dire results always grow from pre-marital sexual relationships. I would fail to display the same fairness and objectivity with which I have asked you to read this volume if I attempted to say that such results inevitably follow. Every young man who knows anything of sexual conduct knows that they do not. There is no way of telling how many instances of intimate relationships occur before marriage without discernible ill effects. Certain individuals who have participated in such relationships express the belief that for themselves the experience has eliminated an obsession or complex in regard to sex which had constantly troubled them. Some feel that they are more objective toward sex as a result of such relationships. The cases of Alfred and Edward illustrate this.

> Alfred—Age 23. College junior. Very interested in literature, music and art. Average scholastic ability and record. Social adjustment above average.
>
> During his sophomore year in college, Alfred adopted intercourse for a short period. He found that it relieved him of the intense desire for sexual relations which he had felt for some time. His ability to consider sexual problems freely and objectively was improved. Later, intercourse as a form of adjustment was dropped, as both Alfred and his fiancée felt that the physical risks involved were too great to warrant the practice.
>
> Edward—Age 24. College student. (Early history on page 43.)
>
> Edward began intercourse when twenty-three years old. The affair was based upon mutual affection. He felt that the relationship had been of considerable value to him in that it satisfied an intense desire, amounting almost to an obsession, for sexual intercourse. This desire probably arose from the strict moral instruction which he had been given at home as a child. The relationship endured for about six months when a change in residence made intercourse impractical, though the

couple continued to see each other. They began to consider marriage, though no definite understanding was reached.

Several months later Edward lost his job. When this occurred his girl berated him as being at fault. Her disappointment was keen—made keener, Edward felt, because of desires aroused by their sexual relationships. To her the loss of his job precluded the possibility of marriage. This created a definite emotional upset. To get away from it she left for a visit. While away, she met a former suitor, a man ten years older than she. After a whirlwind campaign she agreed to marry him.

Upon her return Edward had a conversation with her. To quote him, "After our talk I felt more certain than ever that she was more in love with me than the fellow to whom she is engaged. I feel very much, however, that our affair is chiefly responsible for her contemplated marriage. It kindled in her a desire much stronger than she had ever had before for marriage. I am certainly none too happy over what has occurred."

What position should a young unmarried man take with respect to sexual intercourse before marriage? What is the place of sex in marriage? What answers can be made to those two perplexing questions?

My experience leads me to believe that the only tenable position is that of abstinence. Even in the cases of individuals who felt they had been helped by intercourse the effect was in relation to the individual only. The reaction of the partner, to speak only of the other person most intimately involved, is practically never mentioned. Probably the alteration of individual adjustments in this type of situation is often made at the expense of the other person. The presumption is strong, for example, that this has happened in the case of Edward. Edward himself feels that the affair has hastened the marriage of his partner to a person with whom he believes she is not in love. What the future holds for her cannot be determined but the indications for happiness are none too good. Even Edward himself may have simply exchanged one unsatisfactory adjustment for another no better.

A poor individual adjustment is susceptible of alteration by other ways more likely to achieve desirable results than is intercourse. Repeatedly, individuals have demonstrated that a straightforward discussion of their attitudes with a person who understands problems of sex can produce an improvement. Repeatedly, individuals have demonstrated that sexual relations failed to bring freedom in their approach to sex. Even in cases where improvement is indicated it is an open question as to what produced the change. Quite likely the opportunity to discuss the problem objectively, rather than the actual relationship, was the effective agent. Intense desire for sexual relations may also be satisfactorily handled on other bases than that of immediate satisfaction. One is so uncertain of obtaining the desired reactions, and the possibilities of negative outcomes are so strong that intercourse should definitely be advised against.

The social costs of pre-marital promiscuity have already been discussed. Our society pays a greater price than it realizes for the sexual indulgences of its members. The young man who is interested in living in a society which provides good psychological and sociological conditions for family happiness and a desirable environment for the rearing of children should do all in his power to preserve the social fabric. He cannot expect others to accept the responsibility for creating good social conditions which he himself is unwilling to bear. At the best it seems that only individual adjustment may be altered by pre-marital intercourse. But the effect on social welfare, and long-time outcomes even for the individual all point to the advantages of foregoing sexual intimacies before marriage.

The question "What is the place of sex in marriage?" may be answered with a comment which seems paradoxical and contradictory. In a marriage in which sex is of paramount importance it soon means little. Conversely, when sex means little in a marriage it comes to be a factor greatly contributing to the satisfactions of the relationship. A marriage which is begun largely to secure the satisfaction of basic physical desires, cannot be permanently satisfying. A marriage, if it is to endure, must be based upon something more than biological urges, fundamental as these may be. These urges alone furnish a narrow and shifting foundation.

A marriage entered because the partners have common interests in work, art, reading, recreation, mutual satisfactions resulting from compatible personalities, and above all, the sincere desire to develop and live a rich and complete family life together, has a sound basis for enduring. Sex in the narrow physical sense might practically disappear, and the marriage could continue, rich and satisfying. Yet sex would play an important part, for it would become a way of expressing the satisfaction

[132]

which the partners found in their companionship, and a means of giving and receiving intimate indications of genuine appreciation and affection. The purely physical expression becomes much less important, yet sex in its broader aspect comes to be of much importance.

Sexual relationships within marriage may bear certain very definite functions or values, then, if the partners know how to secure them. The first is the reproductive function. Usually this value is consciously striven for only within marriage, though this function definitely colors attitudes toward sex both within and outside of the marriage relationship. This function is the basis for family life itself, and thus it forms one of the most important of all values. Second, is the function of deriving physical pleasure from sex. This, as has been pointed out, is a desirable value but it must be achieved in such a manner that the individual does not injure other persons or run counter to the general social welfare in satisfying his own wishes. Third, sex may have a definite communicative value. It can serve as a medium whereby each marriage partner may develop an intimate tie and a close relationship—a relationship which will be unique and meaningful only to them. It provides a means of expressing an appreciation and satisfaction which transcend words. Fourth, sex may provide a means of self expression which in turn has a value in personality development. Sex, properly used, provides a method for expressing affection and love. Through this means one is able to indicate one's own attitudes and to afford pleasure and satisfaction to another individual for whom one cares. In the ideal marriage relationship these four factors are combined.

In this sense sex may add much to the beauty of living, but to realize this contribution one must avoid a fixation upon physical pleasure alone. Otherwise this emphasis may prevent one from enjoying sex in its broader, constructive and enriching phases.

PARTIAL SUBLIMATION A FORM OF PRE-MARITAL ADJUSTMENT

The best pre-marital adjustment, in the light of all these considerations, seems to be partial sublimation of the sex desire as described on pages 31 to 40, achieved by interesting, active associations with friends of both sexes. This adjustment is one which can be achieved by young men but adequate recognition must be given the importance of proper surroundings in making it.

Partial sublimation is not a negative adjustment. Nor is it wholly concerned with restraint. It stresses intelligent self-control and the importance of directing interests and desires into constructive channels. The companionship of wide-awake persons of both sexes furnishes concrete help in so adjusting. Stimulating satisfactions can be found in activities other than those of a sexual nature. Desirable sex adjustments entail more than simply standing back and doing nothing.

Probably one of the most serious handicaps a young man faces in an effort to use partial sublimation is the wide range of sexually stimulating factors with which he comes in contact. The attitude and conduct of his associates is one of the most important of these factors.

Adjustment for many a young man would be easier if his associates would drop their constant emphasis upon sex. Often in gatherings of young men, the group attitude tends to stigmatize a virtuous person as a sissy or weakling. The contemptuous label of "male virgin," or "little innocence" makes it difficult for the object of such ridicule to feel at ease when such references are made. Furthermore, if such standards are adhered to by the group members, one who desires to remain with them finds it almost necessary to accept their code.

During this investigation I had several opportunities to observe the effects of group standards upon the behavior of the members. For example, in discussing sex adjustments with several members of a college social fraternity, I found that a large proportion of the young men resorted to prostitution to obtain satisfaction. Various members estimated that approximately nine-tenths of their fraternity brothers did this. Participation seemed to be openly discussed and readily accepted, and no compunctions were felt. One of the fraternity members remarked, "You hear it all the time. Five of the fellows went down to the 'Village' about one o'clock last night. This morning they were up and yelling back and forth in the house about it, and about what a wonderful time they had. You get so you accept it as a matter of course, and feel it is the thing to do."

So strongly is disdain sometimes expressed for those who have not had sexual experiences that the young man who has remained virtuous often feels driven to some kind of defense. He may abandon his self-imposed stand-

[135]

ards and follow the group customs, or pretend, like Vincent, that he is engaging in the same activities.

> Vincent—Age 23. College graduate, intellectually very able. Wide range of boy and girl associates. Honor student. Member of various honor societies. Elected to various positions of leadership.
>
> Vincent belonged to a college fraternity. He soon came to believe that he was the only member of the group who had not experienced sexual intercourse. When it became known that he had not he was subjected to a bit of razzing, which, while by no means barbarous, was nevertheless annoying. Being able to adjust quite well in any group, he found the situation not overly-unpleasant, but soon discovered that it was much easier to let the group assume from his "knowing smile" and assent to their remarks that he, too, was carrying on an affair.

Constant glowing references to casual relationships and intercourse may serve as stimulus to one whose own desires may not previously have been too pressing. Day-by-day association with groups emphasizing sexual topics may arouse the desires so gradually that one fails to realize that it is occurring. Again, it may be a single impressive incident which causes a strong sexual desire to sweep one into a continuous problem of adjustment. Roget's experience is by no means unique. For the early sex history of this outstanding young college graduate, see page 50.

> An incident occurring at age seventeen, though brief in itself, left Roget with a continuous problem of adjustment. One evening a small group of boys, of which

[136]

he was a member, met on the street corner. One of the boys, a little older and the leader of the group, said that he knew two sisters who were staying alone for the evening. He believed that if the group went to them they could induce the sisters to have relations with them. The boys went to the girls' home and failed in their design, but the incident aroused such vigorous desires in Roget—desires he feels, which had already been aroused by masturbation and a struggle which he was then waging against it—that a constant sex urge ensued. The memory of the attempt at intercourse was constantly with him. One night a few months later he overheard plans which indicated that one of the girls would again be alone. He determined to attempt intercourse, even to force the relationship if the girl would not consent. He went to her home, but lost his nerve and nothing came of the attempt. After thinking the incident over he concluded that he had a lucky escape. He decided to avoid further temptations in this direction and in an effort to adjust, tried to build new interests. Adjustment by masturbation was continued.

A knowledge of the psychological and biological factors involved is very important to any young man planning a socially desirable sex adjustment. To separate the two forces in any given case is probably an impossibility since they act together and each affects the other. Experience with young men offers convincing evidence that much of the desire for sexual relations which they find difficult to control is due to stimulating environmental factors.

If an individual is driven to a certain adjustment by

an uncontrollable biological urge, that is one thing. If the biological urge drives him toward the same adjustment because of stimulating factors in the environment, that is another thing—at least as far as control is concerned. Authorities agree that sex has a biological basis. They also agree that sex desires are subject to stimulating forces in the environment. They do not agree that the urge can be satisfied by only one form of adjustment—intercourse, for example.

In conclusion, it is recommended that adjustment be made by partial sublimation with the help of frequent social contacts with plenty of interesting activities between the sexes. Promiscuous and pre-marital intercourse is advised against because of the effect it may have on the welfare of both parties to the relationship. A number of other individuals may be indirectly concerned, and the long-time social effects must be recognized. Some of the more important reasons for avoiding pre-marital intercourse, stated briefly, are:

1. Individual careers are often ruined.
2. It is not yet possible to eliminate all possibility of conception or venereal disease.
3. It often has detrimental effects on one partner though the other may escape completely its effects.
4. Injury often results to those secondarily concerned— members of the family, friends, associates.
5. It may lead to psychological concepts and adjustments which make satisfactory marriage relationships difficult.
6. Long-time social effects are likely to be bad.
   a. The fabric of the family is broken down.

b. Family maladjustments having bad effects, especially on the children, are likely to result.

c. Freedom—or license—demanded by some, leads to a demand for the same freedom for all. This results in our present problems of venereal disease, illegitimate births, and broken homes.

7. The constructive and positive contributions which sex can make to living are likely to be lost as the result of undesirable sex adjustments.

Chapter V

MISCONCEPTIONS IN REGARD TO SEX

So PREVALENT are certain misconceptions concerning sex that practically every person who has received his information by the usual word-of-mouth channels labors under some of them. They are tenacious and obstructive and can be overcome in people's thinking only with difficulty. Some of these misconceptions are discussed briefly in this chapter. An attempt has been made to include only the more common ones. There are many others.

(1) *The misconception that intercourse is necessary to health.* This reason is often given to justify pre-marital sexual intercourse. It has not been reliably determined that persons who have refrained from intercourse suffer impairment of health. Evidence is sometimes offered by quoting statistics showing that married people live longer than unmarried persons. This point loses its force when one realizes that health is an important factor in the selection of a mate. A person in poor health is not as eligible a candidate for marriage as one in good health, and is more likely to decide against entering marriage. Some writers also feel that married people tend to form habits of greater regularity in living, are more hygienic with respect to eating and sleeping, and in a satisfactory

home life find better mental and emotional adjustments. Generally speaking married people, especially men, probably dissipate less than unmarried. These factors, too, may make for greater length of life among married people. So far as health is concerned, the effect of continence or abstinence from sexual intercourse is essentially neutral.

Medical men have at various times indicated their belief that continence is consistent with health. The following statement was signed by 358 representative American physicians:

"In view of the individual and social dangers which spring from the widespread belief that continence may be detrimental to health, and of the fact that municipal toleration of prostitution is sometimes defended on the ground that sexual indulgence is necessary, we, the undersigned, members of the medical profession, testify to our belief that continence has not been shown to be detrimental to health or virility; that there is no evidence of its being inconsistent with the highest physical, mental or moral efficiency; and that it offers the only sure reliance for sexual health outside of marriage."*

On June 7, 1917, the American Medical Association went on record as supporting the following statement: "Sexual continence is compatible with health and is the best prevention of venereal infection."

(2) *The misconception that only weaklings and mollycoddles refrain from intercourse.* The sexual case histories of specific individuals are sufficient to refute this

* Exner, Max J. *The Physician's Answer.* New York: Association Press. 1913.

belief. Young men who are physically and mentally strong and vigorous and who are accepted as excellent examples of masculinity often have not had sexual relations. The case of Alvin, which is found on page 182, illustrates this. Rather than weakness, those refraining from pre-marital intercourse may be showing a marked strength of character. The group attitude sometimes makes necessary a great amount of self-control for the individual to follow a socially desirable code with respect to sexual relations. Individuals sometimes seek intercourse so as to be more readily accepted by the group of which they are a member. Abstinence in a group where relations commonly exist sometimes subjects the individual to a type of bantering which is difficult to take. The easiest course is to observe the customs of your group; to stand against them requires determination and strength.

Some people, both young and old, feel that the youth of today are very promiscuous. The declaration is sometimes made that practically no one is chaste. While there are, without doubt, many individuals who are promiscuous, my work has convinced me that there are many who have not had sex experiences. I have known young people of high character, with excellent reputations and pleasant and dynamic personalities who have habitually followed a chaste and socially approved code of conduct. Many of them have said that often they felt alone and that it was heartening to know that others, too, had accepted similar standards.

(3) *The misconception that the reproductive glands must be used or they will deteriorate.* Deterioration does not occur with failure to use the reproductive glands in

intercourse any more than deterioration occurs by failure to use the tear glands in crying. The testicles function regardless of whether one has intercourse. In an adjustment made without the use of masturbation or intercourse, semen is created and absorbed by the body or ejected in the form of seminal emissions. This misconception is probably much used as a rationalization.

(4) *The misconception that masturbation may result in a variety of ill effects.* This misconception is fully dealt with in Chapter III. A number of references and illustrations were used there to give the facts concerning the supposed ill effects which in the past have been attributed to masturbation. Ellis* writes: "There is really no end to the supposed symptoms and results of masturbation, as given by various medical writers of the last century." He names some of the maladies said to be the result of masturbation. Among these are: insanity, epilepsy, eye disease, headaches, strange sensations at the top of the head, asthma, acne, dilated eye pupils, dark rings around the eyes, functional deafness, red nose, and heart defects of various kinds. He cites one writer who "enumerates and apparently accepts considerably over 100 different morbid conditions as signs and results of masturbation." Medical science, however, has demonstrated that these maladies are not the result of masturbation. Probably one of the most prevalent erroneous ideas is the belief that acne, a skin disease manifesting itself in pimples and eruptions on the face, is the result of masturbation. This affliction is com-

* Ellis, Havelock. *Studies in the Psychology of Sex.* "Auto-Eroticism." Vol. I, Part I. New York City: Random House. 1936. Page 249-250.

mon among young people and to attribute it to auto-erotic practice is to produce needless mental disturbance for many boys.

(5) *The misconception that to cease masturbation it is necessary to have intercourse.* This can be proved erroneous by noting the number of individuals who have stopped masturbation without resorting to intercourse. Ceasing masturbation, as pointed out in Chapter III, may be difficult, but the habit is not necessarily broken if intercourse occurs. In fact masturbation continues in a large proportion of the cases after intercourse. Especially is this true if intercourse is not followed continuously and if masturbation was firmly fixed before it occurred. The most effective method of control is to remove the stimulating factors from the environment.

(6) *The misconception that the sex life is in no way controllable.* This misconception has been dealt with indirectly throughout the discussion. The basis for it is the belief that sex is a biological drive which must be directly satisfied when it is felt. Coupled with this is the belief of many men that they have stronger sex drives than the average. A common statement by young men discussing their sexual urges is that they are over-sexed. Differences in the degree of sexuality among individuals do exist. Thus, in one sense this belief is not erroneous, but the misconception is likely to exist in the individual's belief that he personally is over-sexed. The strength of sexual desires is hard to determine. Secrecy regarding sex is so common that it is difficult to make satisfactory comparisons of one's own desires, urges, and habits with those of anyone else. Problems

[144]

considered in solitude are likely to be magnified. The result is a feeling that one's own sex drive must surely be stronger than those about him.

The excuse of being over-sexed is often used to rationalize a course of sex behavior. It affords a plausible justification for intercourse. Many of those who use it act first, then search for a reason to support their conduct.

Numerous references have been made to aids in achieving self-control. Chapter VI offers a number of suggestions. Many cases have been cited in preceding chapters, and many others could be, to show that control is possible. Particularly is this the case if the individual has a real desire to exercise control.

The following incident illustrates the possibility of altering one's sexual adjustments by deliberate choice. A sophomore in college came to discuss the problem of sexual intercourse before marriage. He and his girl friend had entered upon the practice. For one and one-half hours the question was discussed from all angles, but no decision was reached. A year later, upon meeting the young man, inquiry was made about his decision and his present adjustment. He replied that after thinking over the original conversation carefully, the decision had been to forego intercourse. When asked what measures he had taken to prevent it, he replied with considerable surprise, "Why, I decided it was a good thing to stay away from, and so I just quit. I guess that is all there was to it." There is such a thing as the deliberate decision to exercise self-control, and all of us need occasionally to be reminded of it.

(7) *The misconception that in some respect one is sexually inadequate.* Rather than being a misconception this might better be spoken of as a fear. Sometimes there is a feeling of inferiority arising out of a lack of experience in sexual activities. Young men preparing for marriage have expressed uncertainty about their ability to carry out an act of sexual intercourse.

First of all, the techniques of sexual intercourse are so simple that any physically normal person can readily carry them out. If one has any doubt a careful reading of a book on sexual techniques in marriage, or a conference with a good adviser will give him as much assistance as he needs. Probably the trouble is that such persons are afraid of sex itself, rather than of the actual incident of sexual contact. Some event in their preceding experience, during childhood or adolescence, may have set up inhibitions leading to the difficulty.

In the second place, if the partners to the relationship really care for one another, and are able to discuss their adjustments freely, no difficulty will be experienced in carrying out the act of intercourse. Increasing experience, however, may bring an alteration and refinement of technique and more satisfaction in the relationship.

Still another fear expressed by some persons is that their sexual organs are not of the proper size for intercourse. More men express themselves as afraid they are undersized, than that they are oversized. A reference to the size of the sex organs will be found in chapter II. Hamilton and Macgowan* reported this uncertainty in the group of men they studied. They write, "A sur-

* Hamilton, G. V., and Macgowan, Kenneth, op. cit. Page 193.

[146]

prisingly large number of men have an exaggerated idea of the sex anatomy of their fellows, and consequently believe they are undersized. In answer to a question on this point only fifty-nine men out of a hundred said without reservation that they believed themselves as well developed sexually as most men."

(8) *The misconception that resort to prostitutes is for some persons the solution to the problems of sex.* Prostitution is defined as "the giving or receiving of the body for sexual intercourse for hire, or for indiscriminate sexual intercourse without hire."* This method of satisfying the sex urge is ages old. Every city of size has its quota of prostitutes and houses of prostitution. In some cities prostitution exists outside the pale of the law while in others it is legalized and attempts are made to regulate and control it.

This book can do nothing more than call attention to some of the problems which arise when individuals resort to prostitution. The one of foremost importance is that of health. The contraction of disease is often a result of prostitution. The magnitude of the venereal disease problem is minimized by those who assert that it is being emphasized merely to frighten individuals into the conventional social pattern of conduct. That there is real danger is made clear by abundant evidence coming to light in the campaign recently begun against venereal disease and prostitution.

A book on syphilis written by Thomas Parran,† Sur-

* Woolston, H. B. *Prostitution in the United States.* New York: The Century Company. Page 36. 1921.

† Parran, Thomas. *Shadow on the Land.* New York: Reynal and Hitchcock. 1937.

geon General of the United States Public Health Service, states that 25 per cent of all syphilis cases are contracted by clandestine love affairs and 25 per cent by commercial prostitution. He further points out that the annual increase of newly recognized cases of syphilis in the United States is very high—796 persons in every 100,000 of the total population—when compared to other countries. In Denmark where prostitution was outlawed and suppressed in 1906 the annual increase of new cases is 20 for each 100,000 and in Sweden the rate is 7 for each 100,000 of the population.

An article in the *American Mercury** states that in 1937 there were 683,000 cases of syphilis constantly under treatment; 423,000 new ones arise each year. The statement is made that there are at least 12,000,000 syphilitics in the United States. This means that one person in every ten is infected. That the rate of infection is increasing seems to be indicated by the fact that in New York City the number of persons who sought treatment during the latter part of 1936 was 95 per cent higher than the number receiving treatment during the same period the preceding year. It should be noted that these figures relate only to syphilis.

An assertion frequently made is there is little danger of venereal infection if regular medical inspections are made of houses of prostitution, and certificates testifying to freedom from disease are issued. Experience has shown repeatedly that there is no safety in this method of control. In the first place, even though in-

* Turano, Anthony M. Syphilis: "Mrs. Grundy's Disease." *American Mercury*. April, 1937. 40:400-409.

spections are made, no assurance can be given as to how long the freedom from infection will last. Social diseases are carried readily and every man visiting a prostitute may leave—or take away—the infection. A person engaging in promiscuous relationships runs the risk of contracting the disease with every contact. In the second place, it should be emphasized that certificates are no assurance that the prostitutes were uninfected when the certificate was issued. One should be realistic in this matter. Those responsible for prostitution have never shown any interest in public welfare. According to Parran, and substantiated by evidence collected by the American Social Hygiene Association, investigations have shown repeatedly that certificates are obtained by fraud, out-and-out purchase, hasty and incomplete examinations, or by false statements. A lack of vigorous law enforcement often permits public inspection of brothels to be winked at or entirely overlooked. The authorities, it has been demonstrated, frequently enter into agreements with these establishments. Parran* cites a study made by the American Social Hygiene Association in 1932 in 58 cities, each of the 48 states being represented. It was found that 37 states ignored their laws against commercialized prostitution. This is a worse showing for the control of the practice than was made in a similar study five years earlier. Parran adds, "Medical inspection of the prostitute never has succeeded anywhere in reducing syphilis . . ."

Many of those engaged in prostitution escape any kind of regulation or medical inspection. Recently a

* Parran, Thomas, op. cit. Chapter X.

French physician* wrote, "in Paris there are about 60,-000 unlicensed prostitutes, and only 6,000 at the most who are registered. Furthermore these 6,000 who are licensed form a continually changing personnel. It is rare indeed that a prostitute, after a certain time, does not come to shun police and medical control. . . :

"In fact all doctors who have studied the question in good faith—know full well that licensed houses are an important source of syphilitic and gonorrheal infection. . . . The medical examination of prostitutes, especially when it is done in licensed houses, is usually a farce, pure and simple."

Too much dependence is put upon simple, rule-of-thumb methods of avoiding venereal infection. Simply to cleanse the sexual organs does not insure safety. Infection sometimes results from lesions or breaks in the skin on other parts of the body. Moreover, as I have indicated previously, the individual who devotes himself to promiscuous attachments is almost certain to become careless in protecting himself from infection, and if promiscuity is continued, the almost inevitable result is contraction of venereal disease.

The conditions under which prostitution takes place vulgarize and coarsen sex beyond description. Crude jokes, coarse remarks, and vileness throughout, characterize the atmosphere of such establishments. Not only does prostitution fail to appeal to the finer emotions or to one's aesthetic sense; it is likely also to leave one

* M. le Docteur Rist. "A Physician Discusses the False Security Provided by Licensed Prostitution." *Journal of Social Hygiene.* April, 1937. 23:209-12.

with attitudes which make impossible the wholesome regard for sex which is necessary if it is to become a positive contribution to right living.

One young man, an upper classman in a university,
spoke regretfully of his two experiences of intercourse
with prostitutes. "I didn't know just what was involved
in intercourse so I went in. I'm sorry I ever did. Both
times it was so bestial and animal-like that it sickened
me. I doubt whether I can ever forget the feeling of
coarseness left by the experience."

Frequently young men argue that if the women consent and are paid for giving themselves, the harm has
already been done. They feel that no responsibility is
attached to the actions of the man. Such an attitude
shows little understanding of the traffic in prostitution.
If the brothels are constantly frequented and their ne-
farious business thrives, new girls will be constantly
brought into the traffic, many of them by criminal
devices.

Prostitution as a form of sexual gratification even if
practiced only for a time or two cannot be denounced too
strongly. From every angle the whole business is sordid,
costly, brutal—a curse to public welfare and to individual happiness.

(9) *The misconception that intercourse is to be preferred to masturbation.* This statement is sometimes
given by young men as a justification for their indulgence in intercourse. Two erroneous assumptions are
basic to this belief.

First, that the sex drive must be satisfied either by
masturbation or intercourse. As we have seen in the

preceding discussion, this is a mistaken idea. Physically normal young men are able to make a satisfactory sexual adjustment without resort to either method.

Second, intercourse is assumed to have much less harmful effects than masturbation. This, too, is a misconception. Both the individual and social effects of intercourse—and it is important to keep both in mind —are more harmful than those of masturbation. If either adjustment is to be used as a means of relief, masturbation is much to be preferred.

(10) *The misconception that man cannot control his sex desires as well as woman and therefore needs an especially provided means of satisfaction.* This idea serves as the chief pillar of support for the old double standard of morality. It also gives strong support to the maintenance of prostitution. If man has less ability to control his sex desires than woman, the reasoning is that he is then entitled to greater liberty.

Men living under desirable influences and thinking wholesomely about sex do not find control difficult. The sexual urges and erogenous zones of men, it is true, are more localized than those of women. The sexual organs are more on the surface of the body and, under the influence of stimulation, men are ready for intercourse more quickly than women. The difference, however, is not pronounced enough to require special devices on the part of the male to obtain satisfaction. Rather, the remedy is an understanding of environmental conditions and a willingness to attempt to exercise control.

(11) *The misconception that it is necessary for one to "sow wild oats."* Again the assumption that the sex

urge is a physiological drive which cannot be denied gives rise to this belief. This misconception and others similar to it are in many cases used simply to rationalize desires. The individual holds no sincere belief in the necessity of "sowing wild oats" but because he wishes to do so, uses this as the excuse.

The trouble with experimentation in sex adjustments is that if one makes an improper choice it is very difficult—sometimes impossible—to correct the error. If one brutalizes ones attitude toward sex it is likely to be hard to change it. The long struggle of Roget, pages 50 and 136, to regain a control almost lost, and the feeling of Emmett, page 105, that his promiscuity had decidedly harmed him are cases in point. The experiences of various individuals who have sown "wild oats" should serve as strong deterrents to others who contemplate following their example.

(12) *The misconception that no ill effects can result from intercourse if the girl consents.* This argument should be recognized for what it is in practically all cases —an open plea for freedom and license. As noted above, it is used to minimize the evil effects of prostitution. The girl may have come to accept without hesitancy any approach made, but even so, the social and individual effects of such relationships are still present. She may be consenting without realizing the possible consequences. If she is already so lacking in refinement that no harm to her can result, she is clearly the victim of a system which should be destroyed. Mere consent does not automatically suspend the operation of natural laws or relieve one of responsibility.

[153]

(13) *The misconception that intercourse before marriage is desirable to insure the proper physical adjustment of the sex organs, and to hasten normal sex adjustments in marriage.* This misconception is based upon the belief that sexual incompatibility is the result of improper physical adjustments. Specifically, some believe that the size of the male and female organs has much to do with satisfaction in the sex relationship. They overlook the fact that the vagina, which receives the penis in intercourse, is elastic and in most women will alter in shape to accommodate the male sex organ. Only in rare cases is sexual adjustment seriously affected by the difference in size of the male and female organs.

Similarly, experimentation is said to be necessary to find out whether the male and female orgasm will occur simultaneously. The time of orgasm during intercourse depends upon so many factors that satisfactory adjustment can be achieved only through a long period of experimentation. Emotional conditions, the degree of fatigue, the amount of stimulation, the length of time between intercourse, and similar factors all have an effect. These may be controlled after marriage. Sexual experimentation before marriage tells nothing. Perfect coördination might be secured, in a relationship before marriage, but never again unless due allowance is made for the influence of such factors as those mentioned above.

Sexual incompatibility rises from much deeper causes than mismated sex organs or lack of coördinated orgasms. Couples who find themselves unhappy together because of personal and temperamental differences, be-

[154]

cause their interests are not the same, or because there is no trust or fidelity in the marriage relationship, are likely to find that sexual incompatibility is just one more difficulty added to their already long list. Conversely, couples who are happily matched with respect to these factors find the physical adjustments of sex relatively simple. The wise young man who wishes success in marriage will go far toward insuring it by marrying a girl whose interests, temperament, and personality are compatible with his own. A congenial marriage must be based upon these elements.

Dr. Lewis M. Terman in his recent investigation found data to support the above point of view. He writes,* "In this case the real source of marital unhappiness is not sexual incompatibility *per se* but rather the underlying personality and background factors which have affected the sexual responses. The relationship we have found between happiness scores and sex adjustments scores, to the extent that the relationship is genuine and not due to the rationalizations of the subjects reporting, is probably far more often of psychological than of biological origin. In other words, we believe that sexual incompatibility in the stricter sense of the word is not often a primary cause of marital unhappiness and that what is called sexual incompatibility is in the majority of cases essentially incompatibility of the conditioned personalities."

(14) *The misconception that a display of interest in sex by frank and direct questioning is an indication of maladjustment.* Adequate knowledge and accurate in-

* Terman, Lewis M., op. cit. Page 362.

formation are essential for proper adjustment to the sex urge. A society which affords as many opportunities for sexual stimulation as ours greatly complicates the process of adaptation. While the general attitude often is that anyone indicating an interest in sex is displaying an undesirable tendency or perversion, our society, by its very complexity, makes sufficient knowledge of sex indispensable if a good adjustment is to be obtained.

A few years ago, a large university put a number of books on sex in a special room where young men could have ready access to them. They were little used because, it was said, the idea persisted that anyone seen entering or leaving this room must be struggling with a sex problem. This point of view, fortunately, does not always exist. An interest in sex adjustment, even if it is in relation to an individual problem, can be evidence of a desire to deal with the matter intelligently. Those making the most desirable adjustments are those who, in addition to an objective attitude, have an accurate knowledge of the subject, and a willingness to consider social consequences.

(15) *The misconception that the eating of certain foods will immediately produce sexual excitation.* This is another idea born of ignorance. No foods are sexually stimulating in the sense of producing excitation shortly after eating. The young man who eats a particular kind of food because he thinks it is sexually stimulating puts himself in an excellent frame of mind to feel the reaction he anticipates. The immediate effects of so-called sexually stimulating foods are probably altogether psychological. It is interesting to note that there seem to be

[156]

almost as many "stimulating" foods as there are young men who name them.

Foods which are overly rich, or strongly spiced or which have a disturbing influence on the normal functions of the body may quite likely after a time affect the functioning of the reproductive apparatus along with the rest of the organic system. Some foods contain substances, which when excreted with the urine, irritate the mucous membrane of the bladder and the urethra. This irritation is conducive to sexual stimulation. Good plain foods make for better general physical condition and probably for a more normal functioning of the reproductive system as well as for the entire organism.

Liquors, because of their alcoholic content, make sex control more difficult. This results, not because they are sexually stimulating, but because alcohol destroys the powers of inhibition. Nerve centers are released from normal control and the organism runs wild.

(16) *The misconception that semen given off during an emission or when masturbation occurs has different qualities from that given off during intercourse.* The semen given off in any ejaculation is exactly the same, regardless of the stimulating factor which induced the emission. All semen is produced by the same organs and in the same manner.

(17) *The misconception that a concerted revolt against current standards of sex morality is the solution to the problem.* The issues involved in this statement are far too complex to be adequately discussed here, but a brief comment may not be amiss.

Interestingly enough, the "new freedom" is not a new

idea. From the first civilization ever established upon monogamous principles down to the present there have been periodical revolts against sex restrictions. Waves of liberalism have followed waves of conservatism, and there have even been attempts to establish a social edifice based upon non-monogamous relationships. These experiments have never given evidence of being the correct solution. Nor has the experience of individuals been such as to indicate that extreme liberality is the proper attitude. Of course an attempt at promiscuity in a society where monogamy is the ideal almost certainly is doomed to failure, and the fact that our society has so widely accepted the monogamous standard makes individual experiments in other directions hazardous.

Post-war Russia came as close as any nation could to giving the "new freedom" a trial. With the collapse of the Czarist regime, sex standards changed with the rest. There was a marked increase in promiscuity and freedom in sexual indulgence. Without going into detail, it may be said that Russia found this unsatisfactory and within the last few years has swung steadily toward the more conservative attitude. The same result attended this experiment that has attended others similar to it.

Significantly enough, people who have become recognized authorities in this area of sex deplore the decay of monogamistic standards. They foresee danger for individuals and beyond that danger to society as well.

Hornell Hart* writes, "Fulfillment of personalities in family life depends crucially upon people's being able to trust each other. A sound society cannot be built upon

* Hart, Hornell. *Personality and the Family*. New York City: D. C. Heath and Company. 1935. Page 67.

lies, pretense, hypocrisy, and suspicion. Yet, in a society which punishes as severely as ours does the transgressor of monogamistic mores when he is caught, extramarital sex relations cannot be indulged in without persistent and systematic deception. In our civilization as it is, unconventional sex behavior cannot be practiced frankly, except in rare cases. The average person who engages in illicit relations is practically forced to construct a fabric of lies. This process, of necessity, rots the individual personality, and rots society itself. The person's insincerity, and his knowledge that at any time this false structure may collapse and bring his life crashing down about him, brings mental conflict. The discovery of his falsehoods destroys that confidence on which creative social relations depend. This is not a merely theoretical conclusion. It emerges out of the candid study of actual cases."

In closing his discussion of promiscuous sexual relationships, Hart* says, "All the disintegrative and painful results of extramarital sex relations which have been mentioned above may be traced in great detail in the autobiographical and realistic articles, stories, novels, and plays which are being published currently in great numbers. Tragedy, disillusionment, and cynicism are presented repeatedly, as the outcomes of promiscuous relations, in the writings of persons innocent of any puritanical or religious bias."

The position of Thomas Parran† of the United States

* Hart, Hornell, op. cit. Page 68-69.
† Parran, Thomas. *Shadow on the Land.* New York: Reynal and Hitchcock. 1937. Page 209.

Public Health Service regarding promiscuity is interesting. He writes, "Whatever the causes for the double standard of morals, however, and its encouragement to commercial prostitution, it appears that our present trend to a single standard unhappily is in the direction of the old male standard of promiscuity rather than toward the woman's standard upon which was built the monogamous marriage."

The solution, then, which calls for a revolt against restrictions may be classed as a misconception for two reasons: first, the attempt to alter customs by individuals or small groups cannot succeed in a monogamous society; and second, such experience as has been recorded regarding larger experiments indicates that they are almost certain to fail because they are contrary to sound social practices.

(18) *The misconception that a loss of semen is physically weakening.* The old maxim of the lecturer on sexual topics that "one drop of semen is worth twenty drops of blood" may be suspected as being responsible for this idea. Athletes engaged in strenuous physical sports have been unable to note any debilitating effects from the loss of semen. One writer cites the case of a runner who experienced sexual relations a few hours before one of the strongest races he ever ran. A distinction should be made, however, between a loss of semen, and the possible weakening effects which may occur through a long and protracted incident of sex stimulation. The effect in the latter case is the result of nervous exhaustion growing out of the continuous emotional tension, rather than the loss of semen.

[160]

(19) *The misconception that sex desires are a nuisance which must always be watched carefully lest they elude control.* This misconception comes from a failure to see that sex can play a constructive part in building a well-rounded life. Unfortunately this point of view holds for a large number of people. For example, sex education in the schools, in the few instances in which any instruction at all is given, is too commonly regarded as a safety device—a kind of insurance policy as it were—taken out to prevent immorality and mishap. Sex education properly conceived, should help the individual understand how to utilize sex so as to enrich and beautify life. It should assist him in thinking of this physical attribute as a force with potentialities for grace and magnificence. Yet we still find those who think and speak of the sex urge only as a thing degrading. The solution is not to try to thrust sex out of sight, but to regard it as a natural and desirable force containing wonderful possibilities for increasing life's enduring satisfactions.

The part that sex can play in building family happiness has already been mentioned and will be referred to again in the succeeding chapter. Many young men fail to see the importance of this because they have felt the physical urges of sex, but have never experienced the sexual relationship in a setting in which it was a manifestation of true affection or the expression of a desire for the inauguration of family life. A relationship entered into by two persons who care for each other for the purpose of creating a new life is based upon quite a different set of values from one that is begun solely for physical gratification. It is tragic for a young man to so use sex that he may be deprived of the higher satisfactions of life—to distort into a bane and a curse one of the most ennobling influences of which we have knowledge. There is enough unhappiness in the world which is beyond our control to give us pause before entering into a course of action which can serve only to increase it.

Chapter VI

AIDS IN ACHIEVING DESIRABLE ADJUSTMENTS

SINCE each individual is endowed with the sex drive and must answer for himself—and for society—how he will direct and satisfy this drive, the matter of learning to live with sex is one of prime importance. Each person naturally seeks that mode of adjustment which will bring him and those for whom he cares maximum satisfaction and happiness. In preceding chapters I have tried to indicate what seems the most satisfactory course for young men to follow. This particular chapter will be devoted to suggestions of ways in which this adjustment may be achieved. These are offered with full realization that there are many factors to complicate any particular situation.

Desirable sex adjustments as abstractions are easy to urge, but it is futile to talk about them if they cannot be developed. If one is seeking to adjust in the most satisfactory manner he has a right to ask for as much specific assistance as possible. It is in this spirit that these suggestions are made. Not all possible points are included, only the more important ones. Each person must necessarily select those best suited to his particular situation.

1. *Develop strong and absorbing interests in other fields to supplement the interest in sex.*

This suggestion can probably be of more assistance than any other single one. The person who is busy will find little time to be unwholesomely preoccupied with sex. Hobbies, cultural pursuits, interesting friends, absorbing studies, and the reading of good books will do much to lessen over-emphasis on sex.

Finding varying interests should not be difficult if one is willing to exercise initiative and ingenuity. For active, wide-awake persons, an abundance of opportunities exist. So numerous are the interests which might be followed, each individual will find it necessary to plan for himself. This does not mean that an interest in sex is incompatible with other interests. It does mean that one who is too exclusively concerned with sex is likely to experience difficulties as a result of this preoccupation.

2. *Select friends who will be of assistance in making desirable adjustments.*

Association with friends holding the standards of conduct which you desire to emulate is very helpful. One cannot be constantly with a group holding low standards of sex conduct without finding that problems are raised, especially if one does not wish to accept such standards. Seek instead the friendship of wholesome individuals, particularly those whose interests in sex emphasize desirable standards.

Such friendships should include members of both sexes. To fix attention on members of one sex only is to establish an undesirable unbalance. One may also

[164]

find a satisfaction in cultivating the friendship of persons of varying ages.

An interest in people is probably more helpful in establishing desirable sex adjustments than an interest in things. People of good character react upon their associates. The desire to secure their approval may serve as a powerful motive in establishing and maintaining desirable standards.

3. *Do not be disturbed by manifestations of sex.*

Attention has been called a number of times to the universality of sex urges and desires. In all of my conversations with young men, none has ever denied noticing at times a definite manifestation of sexuality. How disturbing these urges are depends greatly upon individual adjustments. For those who are physically normal, have many interests, and are constantly absorbed in interesting activities, sexual urges are likely to assume a minor place. Every young man will occasionally experience erections, and in practically all cases seminal emissions, no matter how little attention he gives to sex. These should cause no worry to anyone understanding physiological processes.

4. *Develop good habits of physical care, especially regarding exercise, eating, sleeping, and bodily cleanliness.*

The importance of good habits of physical care in exercising, eating, and sleeping was discussed in relation to masturbation. Little further stress need be given here. It is interesting to note that of the young men who were adjusting by partial sublimation many were

[165]

interested in athletics, some participating quite actively. Experience proves that strong, vigorous "he-men" are able to take care of the sex drive by partial sublimation. That good health should facilitate an easy adjustment is logical. Authorities agree upon the importance of good physical habits in securing desirable adjustments.

5. *Do not toy with sex or put yourself in the way of stimulation.*

So many young men fail to realize that easy and normal sex adjustments and constant stimulation of sex urges are incompatible. They hope to hold proper attitudes toward sex and make desirable social adjustments, yet they insist upon continuing lascivious references to sex, seeing sexually stimulating movies, and goading their physical desires by heavy petting or in other ways.

If difficulties with sex adjustments are to be avoided, situations which give rise to the difficulties must be shunned. Some young men seem to feel that they can play with sex, yet exercise control when they wish. Usually little rationality is exhibited by individuals when they are motivated by strongly stimulated sexual desires and it appears possible to satisfy them. They may recall previous resolutions, but generally it is only to cast them aside under the powerful impulse of the moment. The experiences of those who have tried to exercise control in face of marked stimulation is convincing proof that anyone persistently subjected to exciting influences will inevitably meet difficulties in making adequate adjustment.

6. *Plan how you will meet difficult situations before they arise.*

Someone has said that the hardest thing to resist is temptation. Certainly this is true if it comes unawares. In learning to exercise sex control, plan how to meet situations in which control is likely to be necessary. The average youth knows when these are likely to arise. If it is at a dance or the movies, know what procedure will best help you to retain command of your emotions. If problems of control arise in unchaperoned groups, have plans for meeting them. To leave everything to luck is a mistake.

7. *Listen to the advice of those who know.*

The temper of youth is to learn by experience. This is desirable. The difficulty arises when the thing to be learned involves such risk that permanent injury may result to the learner. Since certain phases of sex experimentation involve such danger, one might well, in these cases, consider the wisdom of learning from the experience of others.

Thus, Gilbert, page 104, Maurice, page 126, and Emmett, page 105, testify to the fact that promiscuous intercourse results in attitudes which are likely to jeopardize the chances for happy marriage. The experiences of Anton, page 91, and Joseph, page 103, confirm the belief that there is danger in license. Herman, page 98, found that self-control failed him at the critical moment. Roget, page 136, pointed to the results of an incident which nearly led him into a dangerous indiscretion. Since all these young men were normal, we might reasonably

[167]

expect their difficulties to be duplicated in other normal individuals.

While it is important to listen to the statements of one who seems to know, one should weigh the circumstances under which the statements are made. The boastful stories of exploits related for the benefit of an audience may not represent actual conditions or the true attitude of the speaker. Often individuals assert one thing in a group, but tell a different story privately. Once in speaking to a group of young men I cited figures in regard to the prevalence of masturbation. Later a young man in the audience came to discuss certain matters relating to sex. In the course of the conversation he stated that a friend of his who had also heard the figures had expressed astonishment at the high percentage of those practicing masturbation. His friend added that he himself had only practiced it a few times in his early 'teens, yet a few days later the second young man himself came to ask for more specific suggestions on how to cease masturbation!

Other young men have been known to talk of their exploits with a great deal of bravado, disclaiming any ill effects or regrets arising therefrom. Yet many times in private conversation these same young men have told an entirely different story. Their "bold front" in talking with members of their group changed greatly when in private and serious conversation.

8. *Talk over your questions with someone occasionally. Read worthwhile literature on sex adjustments.*

"Questions" in this case are not meant to refer merely

to worrisome matters of sex, but also to those questions intended to secure ample information for planning a better all around social adjustment. Two investigators* studying the personality adjustment of high school pupils, obtained results which indicated that those with the best personality adjustments expressed more interest in sex than those with poorer adjustments. In their study the pupils who declared they never thought about sex received the lowest scores on the tests and inventories used to measure the status of adjustment. This must be regarded as a tentative conclusion, as the number of individuals included in the investigation was small. But there is ample reason for believing, aside from this investigation, that an expression of active interest in sex adjustment is wholly in harmony with good personal adjustment in other fields.

Talking the whole matter over with an understanding confidant often helps a young, man to take a sensible point of view. This confidant might well be his father, but some other person may do quite as much to help him—a tried and trusted friend, or an older person in whom he can have confidence. Naturally one should select for an adviser some one who can give authentic information, or tell where to get it.

In working with young men I have again and again been impressed with the need each person seems to feel for private discussion and individual assurance. While the answer to the question he asks may have been

* Symonds, Percival M., and Jackson, Claude E. *Measurement of the Personality Adjustments of High School Pupils.* New York City: Bureau of Publications, Teachers College, Columbia University. 1935. Page 23.

[169]

given in a lecture to a group, there seems to be a particular benefit derived from hearing it applied to himself, and to receiving assurance that his special difficulty or one similar to it has been observed in other persons. As a matter of fact, problems of sex adjustment are universal and probably one's own questions are little different from those many others would ask.

The problem of selecting good reading material is important and difficult, since too much of the literature on sexual topics is inaccurate and positively harmful. First, select matter printed by a reputable publishing company. Note the names of the publishers of books listed in the bibliography at the end of this book. Note whether the advertising or the general style in which the book is written is designed to appeal to and stimulate sex desires. Pseudo-psychological magazines or books with lurid titles brought out by obscure publishers will in most cases be found wanting in objective information. They are designed to sell, not to give scientific information.

Second, examine the date of copyright and note the background of the author. Not all old books are poor, but ideas in regard to sex have been changing so rapidly of recent years that a book bearing a copyright date of more than ten or fifteen years ago should be compared with later discussions. The qualifications of the author can sometimes be determined by examining the title page. Here one can often find if he has written other literature in the field, or if he holds a position which might entitle him to speak authentically on the subject.

Third, watch for evidence of bias or one-sidedness in

the author's discussion. Is one phase of sex emphasized to the exclusion of others? Are both individual and social adjustments considered? Are both immediate and long-time effects discussed? Is the presentation moralistic and preachy, rather than objective and direct? A bias, if it does exist, can best be determined by a comparison with the works of several other authors.

9. *Base your friendship with girls on something deeper than physical attraction.*

Youthful love affairs are often said to be opportunities for finding out what qualities one really likes in a friend of the other sex. Certainly this should be true if one is interested in finding a person with whom one wishes to spend the rest of one's life. If a man selects women friends purely on the basis of physical attraction he is likely to find himself much disillusioned in marriage. Those who have chosen their mates by this standard have found that it is far from satisfactory as a measure of other characteristics. It has already been noted that individuals who indulge in considerable promiscuity come to appraise all women from the sexual point of view alone. Personality, educational, and cultural accomplishments go unnoticed.

Associations which rest chiefly on the physical level are likely to be transitory and unsatisfying. A marriage resulting from physical attraction alone faces a strong probability of failure. Terman* concluded from his investigation that if husband and wife were psychologically well mated they were "likely to show a surprising

* Terman, Lewis M., op. cit. Page 376.

tolerance for the things not satisfactory in their sexual relations." Those not psychologically well mated showed no such tolerance. On the contrary they were prone to magnify their sexual difficulties.

The following case, mentioned to illustrate this point, could be multiplied many times. A young couple who had pursued their interests in the physical aspects of sex too far found themselves confronted with a marriage for the sake of expediency. The later comment of the husband was that there were two bases for marriage as he saw it—one real love, the other physical attraction. His marriage based upon the latter was already very unhappy.

To insure desirable friendships with girls, free from over-emphasis upon sex, the association should be based upon as wide variety of interests as possible. Mutual hobbies, a common interest in cultural fields, sports, study, and work all serve to put the friendship on a more enduring foundation. The absence of such interests leaves physical attraction about the only thing the young man and woman can find absorbing.

Often young men ask whether it is preferable to have but one girl friend or several. It is hard to give a categorical answer to this, but in general it seems that there is a period in youth when it is desirable for a boy or girl to establish many contacts with members of the other sex. These associations give an opportunity for appraising the qualities which one finds congenial. Also a number of associations is likely to produce a wide variety of interests and lessen the emphasis on sex which may result from too much intimacy with one person.

10. *Remember that habits change slowly. Start making yourself what you want to be by acting now.*

One of the hardest tasks of the psychologist is to bring people to realize the truth of this. People who have lived maladjusted lives come to him hoping to have their maladjustments cured by the magic of a single conversation, expecting some little device or formula which will wipe the slate clean and allow them to start all over again. Whatever may be the power of psychology, it cannot accomplish miracles. A maladjustment a long time in the making is likely to take an equally long time in correction. The persistence of maladjustments should make any young man weigh all factors carefully before he too readily endangers a good adjustment. Various ones of the case histories found in this book will illustrate this point.

11. *Adopt an attitude that is direct, objective, free from lewdness and obscenity, and that regards sex as a factor which can contribute to richer living.*

Discussions on sex may give helpful and adequate information, and point the way to good adjustment, yet fail entirely because of improper attitudes. Regardless of the amount of information, satisfactory adjustment will not be secured so long as certain habits of reference to sex exist. This means that gutter terminology must be dropped in speech and thought. Lewdness and obscenity must be eschewed and all conversations on sex must be carried on in exact and dignified language.

That sex can be a force to impart a richer quality to life, and provide lasting satisfaction in marriage and

[173]

family relationships has been emphasized repeatedly. There is little to add except that this concept should replace the common attitude that sex is to be indulged in simply for its physical pleasures. When you have accepted this concept you will find you have lost nothing. Rather you will have attained a freedom of thought by which you may utilize this biological urge for adding to the genuine pleasures of life. Not until one can so think of sex is one really free.

12. *Avoid rationalization of your desires. Recognize them for what they are and deal with them honestly.*

Too many times young men seeking advice on problems of sex adjustment are really seeking justification for their actions. In fairness to such persons it may be said that in many instances they are unconscious that this is the case. Fallacious arguments like the following are sometimes, not always, an expression of such rationalizations as these: "I am over-sexed and have a difficult time in controlling my desires," "Man cannot control his sex desires," "It is psychologically harmful to control sex urges," "Everyone must sow his wild oats," "Sex is a biological drive and must be given immediate satisfaction."

If one is really concerned in making a socially desirable adjustment he should examine his points of view to find their origin. Let him ask himself these questions: Am I really sincere in my belief? Is my point of view in any sense a rationalization for a course of conduct I have pursued or want to pursue?

The tendency to find an excuse for what one desires to

[174]

do, then to go ahead and do it is very human. It exists in many fields besides that of sex. Its worst effect is that it destroys clear and logical thinking and thus impedes all efforts toward constructive readjustment.

13. *Remember that the form of adjustment you make is largely up to you.*

,When all is said and done, the fact remains that each must reach his own conclusion. No one else can do it for him. All of the problems—those bound up with the social welfare as well as those which concern only the individual—come finally to rest upon the shoulders of a single person. It is up to him to reach a decision in harmony with the great responsibilities involved.

Chapter VII

DEVELOPMENTAL SEX HISTORIES OF
SELECTED INDIVIDUALS

THE FOLLOWING narrative studies provide a more complete picture of the developmental sex history of individuals than has been given in preceding chapters. This is not an attempt to establish developmental norms. These cases are for the purpose of indicating the universality of the sex urge, the frequency with which a maturing boy meets questions relating to sex, and of showing how certain persons have met them. Attention is called to significant features which will be of help in securing a more comprehensive knowledge of the influences which affect the sexual attitudes and adjustments of the average young man.

The history of Ames is that of a boy who grew up with practically no guidance in sexual matters. He drifted along, bumping into first one phase of sex and then another, never knowing just what he was about to encounter, or how to meet the situations as they arose. He has been considerably influenced by men and boys older than himself.

> Ames—Age 18. University sophomore. Very capable intellectually. Above average student. Social adjustment satisfactory.

When about five years of age Ames remembers being with a group of boys, some older than himself, when a conversation took place concerning sex. The discussion centered on the way reproduction occurs and birth takes place. Ames heard it with amazement and incredulity. This was his first awareness of sex.

He can remember nothing further until about ten years of age when he and a little girl examined each other's bodies to notice the difference in structure. The only motivation was curiosity. Shortly after this he came more directly in contact with older fellows who talked with each other and with him concerning sexual matters. These conversations played an important part in awakening his sexual curiosity, and he began to search for more information. Sex occupied his mind, he read what he could find on the subject, and engaged in salacious conversations in order to learn more about it.

In addition to these older associates, Ames at the same time had friends in a group of boys about his own age. This group would occasionally drift into discussions of sexual topics and on one occasion made an examination of their reproductive organs. Ames participated, but the incident was revolting to him. Subsequently it was repeated several times by the group when they found themselves in a secluded spot, relaxed and possibly tired, but Ames never took part in it again. His home training had left him with a vague feeling that such conduct was reprehensible.

One other incident of sexual behavior left a definite impression upon him. When about thirteen years old, he and four older boys were at a "kid clubhouse" together. The other boys suggested a contest to see who could complete masturbation first. This was Ames' first

[177]

masturbatory experience and he found some enjoyment in the act. Afterwards he felt a revulsion against it and dropped associations with the other fellows. But about this time he began to masturbate regularly, practicing it with variations in frequency for three years. The range was from three times a week to once a week, or once every two weeks.

One evening, when about sixteen years of age, he went for a ride with two older boys, neither of whom bore a good reputation. On the ride they picked up two girls who had equally poor records of conduct. Ames recognized that he was in a distasteful situation, but hoped no untoward incident would occur. The other members of the party evidently noticed his discomfiture, and took measures to increase his embarrassment. A period of "heavy petting" followed, after which intercourse occurred. Ames was ridiculed by the other members of the party until he, too, participated. Afterwards he was considerably distressed for fear he might have contracted a venereal disease.

Ames is definitely opposed to pre-marital relations. In fact in the two years since the incident mentioned above he has had little to do with girls. He still feels a sense of shame and embarrassment over some of his sexual experiences. Masturbation now occurs infrequently—six or seven times a year—usually following some reading or conversation which has produced sexual stimulation.

Ames feels that he has received very poor assistance in making sexual adjustments. His parents have given him no help at all. He can recall his mother telling his father at different times that he should, "tell the boys what they ought to know." His response was that they were too young. Ames' single source of authentic information was a biology course in high school. This provided some help but not enough, since no one in the class, instructor or pupils, felt able to talk freely. Ames feels that from the beginning his whole experience has been that of running into one sexual incident after another and finding himself entirely unprepared to cope with any of them. The only help other than the course mentioned has been what he could provide for himself, through bits of reading picked up here and there.

Garrett is another whose adjustment has been considerably influenced by his early experiences. The constant association of sex with sensuality left him psychologically vulnerable to the allurements of an older woman. Once having participated in sexual relationships it was easy to seek further affairs. This is the case history of a young man who, once having overleapt the barriers which kept him from heterosexual activities, became more and more promiscuous.

Garrett was reared in a home broken by divorce when he was about six years of age. As he now knows the story, his father was promiscuous in his sexual relationships after marriage. Because of this his mother refused to live with him, and after a period of emotional stress sought divorce. Garrett was first given into the custody of his mother, and later, after his father's remarriage, into that of his father. He feels that this situation has definitely influenced his later conduct. It is quite likely that his parents have passed on to him their own sexual maladjustments. The fulfillment of Garrett's expressed

[179]

desire for a home and family life superior to those of his childhood probably depends in a large part upon his ability to make a socially desirable adjustment to sex.

Garrett—Age 21. College sophomore. Average student. Well liked by associates. Interested in athletics.

Garrett can first remember an awareness of sex about the age of five. At that time curiosity in regard to sexual differences led him to examine the anatomy of a little girl who lived in the neighborhood. This instance is particularly vivid because Garrett's mother came across him during the procedure. He was whipped and warned not to do it again, though no reason was given for regarding his conduct as undesirable. Garrett believes that the punishment served only to heighten his curiosity and make him more wary. After this he tried further to satisfy his curiosity by following older boys to the lavatory. Sometimes the older boys, observing his interest, would perform acts with sexual implications.

From age seven to twelve Garrett played with a group of boys who used a hut as a gathering place. Here there was a good bit of discussion of sexual topics in which each boy exchanged his bit of information with the others. Examination of sex organs and mutual sex play was common. In a few instances girls were brought to the hut. At these times mutual sex play and examination of organs occurred. There was also much talk which served to stimulate sex desires.

During his freshman year in high school, Garrett and a friend with whom he often slept, found a good deal of pleasure in homosexual activities. These instances were infrequent, occurring only about five times in all. They took place on occasions when the boys were alone or spending the night together. Usually, this mutual sex play was accompanied by talk of intercourse, seduction of girls, and similar topics. Neither Garrett nor his friend have resorted to homosexual activities since, though they feel no regret over the times they did.

Garrett received rather extensive information from his mother, a trained nurse who described for him the anatomical differences between men and women, and explained something of their physical relationships to one another. Also she warned him against masturbation and venereal diseases but nothing she told him proved of any help in building ideals in regard to sex or in any way ordering his sexual relationships with boys and girls.

Masturbation began at twelve, growing out of the curiosity aroused by his previous conversations with his friends, as far as Garrett can remember. He was spasmodic in his practice of it. Sometimes it occurred daily for three or four days. Then a week might elapse after which there would again be a clustering of incidents. At twenty-one it is still practiced. The frequency now is about once every two weeks. Garrett finds that it usually occurs on a week-end when he is less busily engaged than at other times. After a petting party, some particularly stimulating incident or sexual phantasy, masturbation is often used to secure release. There is also a certain amount of physical pleasure in the act which leads Garrett to continue it.

When seventeen years of age, he accompanied his step-mother, father, and sister on an extended sea cruise. With them was an older divorced woman, a close friend of his step-mother. She was well educated and in the eyes of the family a woman of high moral principles. During the trip she and Garrett became increasingly intimate. She conducted herself so that he became aware of her sexual desires. Being inexperienced, he was not very aggressive, but during the latter part of the vacation she opened the way for sexual intimacies and created the opportunity for them. Following the initial experience coitus occurred a number of times. At the close of the trip the association was broken, and Garrett has not seen the woman since.

This initiation created an active desire for further heterosexual experience. After his return he renewed his acquaintance with a former girl friend, and in a short time induced her to participate in sexual relations. Following this he carried on affairs with eight other girls for varying lengths of time. During the summer of his twentieth year, he became associated with a group where sexual promiscuity was the accepted behavior and had relationships with seven different persons, all of them casual acquaintances.

After the summer's experiences he began to wonder whether his conduct might be building habits which would later lead to difficulty in marriage. He himself is the product of a broken home and feels that his adjustments are a direct result of his home environment. A number of other adjustmental difficulties besides those of a sexual nature have grown out of the situation, and since Garrett hopes eventually to have a home of his own which is stable and harmonious he is interested in doing what is necessary to insure it.

The ease of adjustment experienced by Alvin has been largely due to his excellent home environment and his active and interesting school, social, and athletic career. His experience encourages one to believe that with a good home and absorbing activities, wholesome adjust-ments to sex can readily be made. His experience also indicates that sexual abstinence is in no wise inconsist-ent with masculinity, a position of respect in school and community, and general satisfaction with life. The chance of his making a superior and happy adjustment to marriage and family life should be considerably above average. Sex should continue to serve as a constructive, enriching force in his life.

Alvin—Age 22. University senior. Three-letter man in football. Elected to various leading student offices. Honor student. Three times class president during his university career. Highly respected by both students and faculty. Character excellent.

Alvin has accomplished a remarkably easy adjust-ment to sex. It seems that he grew very gradually into awareness of it. He has never masturbated nor had sexual intercourse. Seminal emissions occur about every two weeks, and he has occasional physical manifesta-tions of sex desires. He has had the usual associations with girls since he was about fourteen years of age. For three years he has been going with one girl to whom he is engaged.

Alvin feels that his easy adjustment has been achieved largely because of his home influence, and because of his wide range of interests. While his parents have never discussed sex openly with him, he has well un-derstood their standards of morality, and has felt them to be right. He has the highest admiration for both his mother and father. His father, he feels, is one of the most moral and upright men he has ever known. His

[183]

home has always been harmonious and pleasant, and the associations in it uplifting.

Ever since he was a small boy, Alvin has been active in athletics and school affairs. He had a tennis court at his home and belonged to a church group and a boys' club where he could participate in sports of all kinds. During his college career he has made four letters in varsity sports. He has served as president of his class for three consecutive years. His school work has always been interesting, and has occupied a good share of his time. He has always taken part in church work and young people's groups.

Alvin has read articles and books in regard to sex and has adequate information for making his adjustments, though his fund of technical information is not large. For two years following his high school graduation he worked with a construction gang. Here he heard a great deal of discussion of sexual topics but because he was busy and because of his previous good adjustment these conversations afforded no stimulation.

Alvin and his fiancée plan to postpone intercourse until after marriage. There are physical expressions of affection between the two, but they are careful to avoid making them over-intimate or prolonged. Alvin finds that they produce no sexual stimulation except occasionally when he may experience an erection following a good-night embrace and kiss. Alvin feels that the definite intention of himself and his fiancée to order their courtship so that stimulation does not result from their associations has done much to make things easy.

The developmental history of Philip illustrates two interesting points. First, the chance way in which he learned masturbation indicates that, without one's realizing it, sex may be closely associated with other apparently unrelated phases of living. Second, the extensive use of petting, following a period barren of the usual associations with girls, points to the need for an ordered, natural type of social activity including members of both sexes. What was true for Philip is equally true for other young men. That men who have long been deprived of normal heterosexual associations often go to excess in their indulgences is commonly known.

Philip—Age 22. College junior. Above average student. Leader of boys' groups. Mature and objective in thinking for his age.

Philip's first information in regard to sex was received when he was about five years of age. He asked his mother to explain the origin of his navel. She explained for him, in a vague way, the birth of a baby. The explanation was so hazy, however, that Philip grew up thinking that a baby was delivered by way of the mother's navel. This misconception gave rise to a curiosity which caused him to seek further information. The dictionary, an obstetrician's manual, and other books unearthed from dusty stacks in the attic, all contributed to his knowledge.

Masturbation began about fifteen. Philip learned of it one day during a hike when the tightness of his clothing produced an erection, then a climax and seminal emission. After this he was easily able to continue masturbation. The act, once begun, occurred as frequently as once and sometimes twice daily for about a year and a half. The frequency gradually dropped to once a week, and it is now about three or four times yearly.

Philip's experience with girls did not begin under

the most favorable conditions. While he was in grammar school, before he was adequately informed about matters of sex, some of his classmates asserted that they had seen him engaged in intercourse with a girl whom "everyone knew about." Philip was extremely embarrassed by this unwarranted accusation and responded to it by "steering clear" of girls in general for the next five years.

When a junior in high school he had a puppy love affair and went through the pangs of being jilted. Following this he entered upon a series of more or less serious attachments. He went with several girls successively, regarding each as his "one and only" until he realized that his fidelity was not reciprocated. Since then Philip has usually kept from three to five girls "on the string." His dates usually consist of a drive, a movie, a concert or similar amusement, often followed by a petting party. For Philip that usually means excitation and stimulation to the point of emission.

The use of petting as a form of sexual excitation occurs chiefly during summer vacations, college vacations, and on week-ends. Philip has found the most intensive use of this practice as a form of adjustment follows intervals when he has been deprived of normal associations with girls. As an example he cited a period following his return from a military training camp where he had had no associations with girls. Within ten days he had had several petting episodes with each of three different girls.

Philip thus far has avoided intercourse. His plans preclude marriage until he is thirty years old. He may remain abstinent until then but would be ready to accept sexual relationships if he found someone for whom he cared a great deal.

The case history of Carter is a good illustration of the unwholesome sex education which all too often comes when one is obliged to work in the midst of unpropitious surroundings. He went forth entirely unprepared by parents who either could not or would not give him adequate instruction. His association with persons who themselves were lascivious, lewd, and promiscuous had a profound effect on his later adjustment.

The lack of balance in the information which he received is a common feature of the sex instruction which boys are given. A sex education program to be of practical value to boys and girls must be directed by someone who knows the actual problems they are likely to meet, and is able to talk to them in terms of these problems. To confine the teaching to a description of the sex organs, a few vague warnings, and prophylactic information is entirely inadequate.

Carter—Age 23. University sophomore. Active in athletics. Above average in scholarship. Social adjustment satisfactory.

The earliest sexual impressions which Carter can recall arose from an incident which occurred when he was about nine years of age. A group of children, boys and girls, playing in an attic, disrobed in order to examine their anatomical differences. The incident did not make a very marked impression on Carter.

Much more important were the teachings he received while working in a mill from the older hands. Much talk was bandied about concerning intercourse and marriage. Carter received a perverted impression of sexual relations between men and women. They seemed coarse and vulgar, and he can remember that for a time his parents were lowered in his estimation.

He also learned masturbation from the mill hands and practiced it about once a week from age thirteen to age seventeen. Since then it has occurred infrequently. Sexual intercourse occurred at seventeen and grew out of an affair initiated and nurtured by a girl five years older than Carter. This association lasted for about a year. Since then Carter has had coitus a number of times and with eight different persons.

When he was twenty years old Carter accompanied a group of young men to a house of prostitution. After they arrived he decided not to take part in the proceedings, but under persuasion finally succumbed. He returned to the house once again, but was so disgusted that he never went back. Now he says he is sorry that he ever went in the first place, since the two experiences placed sex on such a low and bestial plane that he has never quite been able to overcome a feeling that here is where it belongs.

Carter never received any sex instruction in his home. In high school he heard the physical features of human reproduction discussed in a very formal and impersonal way. Nothing was said about the practical problems of sex behavior. In a hospital where he worked for a time he met a young physician who gave him information about prophylaxis and contraceptives, but this was of little aid in adjustment, since the physician described his own affairs with women in such a way as to stimulate Carter to secure further intercourse himself.

The effects of a poor educational program is also indicated in the case of Marion. His first awareness of sex was made unusually vivid as a result of a lecture which he received and his respect for the authority of the older man. At the same time strongly emotionalized attitudes were set up and standards of conduct created which, so far as he was concerned, were not based upon fact or reason. All this resulted in a conflict which has influenced his whole adjustment to sex and his relations with his associates. The attempt to resolve this conflict without guidance is reflected in the incident occurring in his nineteenth year. So strongly has the whole issue colored his thinking that there is even yet a feeling of uncertainty as to what his adjustment should be and whether he is "like other fellows."

Marion—Age 21. College senior. Above average student. Good character. Closely affiliated with church activities. Well liked by most of his associates. Active in school affairs.

Marion's first awareness of sex came at the age of seven. At that time he was instructed by an older man never to "play with himself," to avoid such associations with any other boys, and not play with girls. These admonitions were given in such a way as to create a very vivid impression. A feeling of repugnance for any kind of sexual activity resulted. So strong an inhibition was built that Marion has always found it difficult even to talk with other individuals his own age about sex. He has never found it possible to handle his own sex organs, or in any way participate in sex activities with others.

The next vivid impression came when he was about thirteen or fourteen years old. One day after a sandlot baseball game a group of older fellows began a conversation on sex with Marion and some of his friends. Information of a vulgar nature concerning intercourse,

[189]

conception, and birth was given. These were the first facts of this nature that Marion had ever heard and they left him utterly amazed and upset. For a long time he was unable to reconcile such behavior with the conduct of nice people. Even now, at age twenty-one, he finds himself embarrassed by discussions of sex and ill at ease in a group of young men where it is a topic of conversation.

Marion has never received any instruction on sexual matters from his father, though when sixteen he asked an older friend about seminal emissions and received information in a wholesome way. Also he secured reading material from his local Y.M.C.A. and from the high school biology course.

Marion has never masturbated. The feeling of loathing for it created by the warning he received still persists. Also Marion dislikes any sexual phantasies or mental dalliance with sex and is, on the whole, free from anything of this nature. Seminal emissions occur about as with the average youth.

So keenly has Marion felt the conflict between his standards of conduct and the codes of behavior of his fellows that he is always on the defensive with them. To rid himself of this feeling, at age nineteen, he agreed with a worldly-wise associate to have intercourse with a girl whom this person knew to be readily susceptible. After the girl had been informed concerning Marion's purpose in meeting her, they had two dates. On the first Marion found himself unable to make advances, but on the second, with the girl's encouragement, he showed more aggressiveness and reached the point of intercourse. At this stage he was so overcome with disgust that he insulted the girl and withdrew. A little later he tried to carry through the act with another girl under similar circumstances. Again he found himself unable to meet the situation. Marion still feels ashamed of these episodes and finds difficulty in discussing them.

Friends and associates have always regarded Marion as puritanical, prudish, and somewhat superior in his attitude regarding sex. Marion feels that this grows out of his inability to meet his contemporaries on their own grounds. In his embarrassment when sex is discussed, about the only thing he can think of to do is to make a remark about "matters of this sort" being on too low a plane for his attention and swing out of the room.

Marion feels quite strongly about the difficulty which he has experienced because of his early misinformation and his more or less irrational outlook. He declares with feeling that if he ever has anything to do with school or the development of educational programs for children or young people he is going to see that there is a thorough-going program of sex education.

An interesting variation in the problem of sex adjustment is found in the case of Neil. While his difficulty is manifested in a different manner from those of other individuals mentioned in this book, the roots are of common origin. His parents attempted to enforce a code of strict sexual morality upon him without a clear understanding on his part of the reasons for the standards. This brought on a disturbing conflict between the code of the home and of persons outside the home. Neil could certainly have been saved much of his perplexity and worry if he had been widely and wisely informed.

Neil—Age 20. College freshman. Excellent character.

Mental ability and scholastic record above average. Social adjustment satisfactory.

The first knowledge Neil had of sex came several years before maturity from conversations with his friends and bits of information picked up here and there. He had very little contacts with sex before maturity and as far as he can remember these conversations outside the home had little effect on him. He received little information, chiefly warnings against intercourse and masturbation from his parents, though they did succeed in securing his temporary acceptance of a very strict moral code in sexual matters.

After maturity was attained about the age of thirteen, Neil began to take more interest in girls and social activities involving members of both sexes. During these associations he saw a distinct contradiction between the standards which had been taught by his parents and the standards of his group as exemplified in their speech and sometimes in their actions. Conversations about sex and knowledge of sexual episodes tended to create in him very strong sexual desires. As a result he found that almost any contact with girls, even the most casual, and any reference to sex in reading, movies, or conversation induced strong sexual excitement. These instances of excitation occurred every night and usually two or three times during the day. Also he found much mental imagery of a sexual nature accompanying excitation. This stimulation was manifested particularly in erections and marked physical desires for sexual relations.

So frequent and so pronounced was the difficulty that Neil often wore an athletic supporter to hide the physical aspects of the erection which occurred during class time, when in a group, whether entirely male or mixed, or when at work. The supporter was worn most during the two or three years following maturity.

At night after retiring the problem was particularly annoying. Sleep often was long delayed because of sexual excitement; sometimes it was impossible until after masturbation. The same thing occurred in the morning unless he arose promptly. He began masturbating shortly after sex maturity, largely to secure relief from the intense stimulation and accompanying physical discomfort which he so frequently experienced. At first he tried to resist the desire to masturbate but the practice continued. The frequency ranged from once to twice a week. Seminal emissions practically never occurred.

Neil felt ashamed and worried about his adjustment. He was afraid it was leaving him with a distorted view in regard to the whole problem of sex, and making his control when in contact with girls very difficult. He had indulged in petting to some extent, and while he desired to avoid intercourse, he was fearful that at some time when excited, his desires and passions would completely overcome his control. He fought masturbation and the frequent sexual excitation, but was unable to make any headway in gaining mastery over them. His standards of conduct and morality, as he expressed them, were commendably high.

Six months after Neil's discussion of his difficulties he left home to attend a large college. Here he was associated with boys who were engaged in a wide variety of absorbing activities. He found that under the new influences his sexual difficulties all but disappeared. On a few occasions he noticed erections but these came with

[193]

decreasing frequency. Also masturbation was dropped to a frequency of once every two weeks and his whole attitude changed to one of confidence in his ability to handle the problems of adjustment satisfactorily.

The following history, supplied by Norman, illustrates a state of mind growing out of lack of sound information. With adequate instruction and proper guidance, a satisfactory adjustment should have been relatively easy for a young man with his moral standards, high ideals, and mental capacity.

The history is left in the first person as he prepared it so that his attitude toward sex and toward his parents, as well as his needless difficulties with adjustment, may be better indicated.

Norman—Age 23. University graduate. Honor student. Very active in extra-curricular activities. Capacity for leadership. President of student government organization. Active in church organizations. Preparing for social and religious work with boys and young people. Recognized as being of good character.

"My first information in regard to sex came when at eight years of age I was told the story of birth by my mother. It was beautifully told, and I shall always have a lovely picture of this subject. 'In mother's body,' she said, 'is a small nest—much like the nest of a bird. It is there you began as a little thing, and you grew until you were able to live alone—just as the bird stays in the egg until it is able to come out into the world.' And the story continued in this tenor.

"The *only* other training I got was punishment on one occasion. Once I spent a long evening with a girl, in her back yard, talking to her. She was the girl friend of my friend and I didn't touch her for I was very idealistic about those things. But the late hour worried my mother, and when I returned I got no word—only a swift slap on my face. I realized vaguely that she was concerned deeply about my relationship with the girl, and I wondered what terrible things boys and girls of my group did. It is true that I knew of sexual intercourse at the time, but it was so remote!

"My home training produced only perversion and difficulty. Sheer ignorance caused me no end of trouble and worry. I could have met problems of boy-girl relationships much better and with much more confidence had my parents been sensible about sex education.

"From very earliest boyhood I was conscious of my sex organs as a source of stimulation. From the time I can remember I used to press them against the bed clothing to produce physical contentment and pleasure before falling asleep. At five or six, several other small boys and I entertained ourselves almost daily exposing our sex organs for mutual amusement. My brother, my boy friend, and I used to undress before each other in the attic. At eight or nine my small cousin, a girl, used to join me surreptitiously and together we would compare organs. I also developed a friendship with another boy and his sister about this time, and the boy and I would compare our sex organs and otherwise exhibit ourselves before his sister.

"At fifteen years of age an unusual experience occurred which frightened me. Having heard nothing informative of sex either from my mother or from my friends I was not aware either of sexual intercourse or masturbation. But one night as I lay in bed I had the

[195]

usual erection. And without previous instruction or suggestion I practiced masturbation. The sensation and the emission of semen frightened me, and I ran to the bathroom—thinking I had to urinate! I worried that night, and the next day I went to my boy friend and asked him about it. He, I found, masturbated twice a day! I finished my fifteenth year better than he, for I held to an average of once a day.

"My brother knew I was having trouble, and he shyly told me of masturbation, and advised me to stop it—I couldn't.

"Until I was nineteen years of age, due to fear and ignorance and a strong touch of inferiority complex, I never kissed a girl. Holding hands was my only indulgence. I increased my knowledge of girls, however, through my imagination and the use of pictures which I had before me during my evening masturbations.

"After high school graduation I began to discipline myself; I managed to cut down the masturbation to every other day through daily entries in a diary or journal. During this period I met a girl, and through her gained some of the necessary feeling of superiority. I even kissed her! The only other physical contact was holding her close to my body; never with her did I become stimulated or indulge in physical exploration.

"It wasn't until I entered the university that I began to learn 'the score.' Bull sessions began it, and I decided to find out a few things. But I fell madly in love with a decent girl and we held to kissing each other goodnight. But she, like me, was curious too, and we progressed very slowly from lips to physical explorations until within a year I knew the feminine body quite well! In our sophomore year I reduced masturbation to once a week. On Saturday nights we would indulge in petting for hours and I would quietly end the experience on the side with masturbation.

"This unnatural condition was not satisfactory to the girl and irritation broke up the relationship our junior year. Still ignorant of too much, I gave up in disgust, returned to 'virtue,' and chose a quiet, unsophisticated and inexperienced girl for the remainder of my college life. Deliberately I tied myself to her, kissing and embracing her—no more. Three times within the year and a half opportunity presented itself during petting episodes for masturbation but it was rather inconvenient! So I satisfied myself with masturbation alone, in my room at intervals of, I suppose to be honest, every three days on an average. At one time I went a month and three days, but the intense pain drove me to masturbation.

"Today, through with my university course, I am unable to have any contacts with girls as I am out of work. Masturbation is more frequent and I am seriously considering finding the right girl and having intercourse before marriage. Admitted ignorance and inability to discuss the matter with my parents holds me in stalemate, however.

"So that today, I am a victim of the wide spread lack of sex education. My imagination has played out, and masturbation is cold—I am ready to enter into premarital sexual relationships and, without knowledge, I may get into trouble. I find myself looking for attractive girls from the window of my home and practicing masturbation at that time. I realize that this is the slow road to perversion; that is why I write this report, hoping that in return I may get helpful advice."

The following note was enclosed by Norman with his report:

"I hope this brief discussion will be of help to you. Frankly I made the offer to send you this material because I do need help in an educational way. Being out of work I can't afford to send away for instruction, and even then you never know what you are getting.

"Rest assured that I have no predetermined ideas or perversions on the subject. I want only to do the best thing in the light of scientific adjustment. I must go another four years before marriage is possible, and masturbation has played itself out.

"I trust your secrecy with respect to any member of my family, not to make even the slightest allusion to my situation. Write to me, and be quite frank, as you have been, and as I have tried to be in the letter and report."

The baneful effects of some of the experiences met by young men at work are well illustrated in the case of Milton. Perhaps it is true that some types of work afford more opportunity for unwholesome experiences than others. Yet one cannot always be sheltered from awareness or even from contact with such experiences. The best safeguard for any individual is a careful education in regard to sexual matters and specific help and suggestions about how to meet such situations as may arise. In this case, as in others, the existence of a confidential relationship between a young man and a sympathetic, understanding older person would be a valuable aid. No one should be surprised by Milton's failure to discuss his experiences with his parents.

Milton—Age 21. University junior. Intellectually

above average. A leader in various student activities. Social adjustments satisfactory.

The first distinct memory Milton has of sex came from an incident occurring when he was about eleven years old. One day following a game with a group, one of the older boys masturbated and told Milton that he should try it, as it was a very pleasurable experience. Milton was non-committal and uninterested. He can recall no particular effect induced by the episode. About two years later he met another boy his own age who introduced him to masturbation for the second time. Milton was now sexually mature, and as a result of this contact he began the practice. It occurred a number of times in the company of his friend, though the frequency was only about once a week.

At the time Milton was associated with a group of boys who indulged in vulgar and lewd conversation. He remembers particularly the stimulating situation which he and members of his group produced during one school year when they had a teacher whose manner of dress and conduct provided a constant topic of conversation for them.

No information on sexual matters was ever given Milton by his parents. He has never talked to them about anything relating to the subject. He can remember only a salacious reference to intercourse made by his brother. This occurred under circumstances which induced sexual desires for Milton rather than offering him any assistance. He secured no authentic information and help until his freshman year in the university.

When about seventeen years of age, he secured a job as a musician in a traveling jazz orchestra. Here he was associated with a group whose sexual conduct was loose and promiscuous. They found and created frequent opportunities for participation in sexual relations. A good deal of pride and rivalry was exhibited by the various members in the number of conquests they had made. The leader in such activities was designated as "Wolf No. 1," the person with the next highest number of episodes as "Wolf No. 2," and so on.

During the year and a half he was with the organization Milton accepted their attitude, but did not participate widely in actual sexual activities. However, his first experience in intercourse occurred during this time with a girl who, he feels, was probably a prostitute. Later he had relations with another girl. During this whole time he experienced a great deal of sexual stimulation. Masturbation reached its highest frequency, about three times a week. He was careful to keep the whole matter from his parents.

Milton quit the orchestra to enter the university. The knowledge of sexual adjustments which he received here caused him to resolve to forego further intercourse. He later became acquainted with a girl with whom he felt he could have had coitus had he desired and dropped the friendship to avoid such a culmination. Milton has dated various girls regularly during the last three years. He adjusts pretty largely by normal associations with members of both sexes and by seminal emissions. Masturbation occurs every month or two.

Well-intentioned parents unable to give their son adequate guidance play an important role in the developmental history of Hayes. The itinerant and promiscuous worker who provided him with his first patterns of sex conduct performed the function of the parents. The beneficial effects of the positive attitude of the well-adjusted counselor, together with Hayes' analytical mind and tendency to think all issues through, illustrate what can be done to direct an improved adjustment to sex.

Hayes—Age 22. College junior. Very able intellectually. Considerably above average in scholarship. Leader in school activities.

Hayes can remember no particularly outstanding instances of a sexual nature in his early life. His only memories are of seeing his sister undressed, hearing some of the neighbor boys commenting on clandestine relationships involving certain persons in the vicinity, and events of a similar kind. Everything was pretty much on this level until about fifteen years of age when he began work in a garage during time off from school. Here he became acquainted with older boys and men whose chief topic of conversation was the lewd and sensual aspects which they saw in sex. Hayes listened with a feeling of awe and fascination. As he recalls it, it seemed to him that at first he could never hear enough. He carried the information he got from them back to his own group where he led "bull sessions" on sex topics.

Looking back Hayes can see distinctly how the sensuality and general disrespect for women evidenced by his associates gradually permeated his own thinking until he became like them. Masturbation began about sixteen, though it did not occur more than two or three times a month. According to Hayes and his associates, masturbation was vicious and unmanly. Intercourse was the end to be striven for.

[201]

Since intercourse was so strongly recommended, Hayes began to seek an opportunity to participate in it. His first chance came when he was about eighteen when he had relations with a girl friend, an acquaintance of long standing. Their affair lasted for a year, intercourse occurring a number of times during this period. In the succeeding year Hayes had relations with three other girls.

While carrying on one of his affairs Hayes overlooked some contraceptives, leaving them in a pocket of his suit where they were found by his mother when she was sending the clothes to a cleaner. She gave them to Hayes' father, who returned them to him the same evening. As he handed them to Hayes he remarked that Hayes should remember that he had sisters living in the house. The impression Hayes received was that his father did not mind if he participated in sexual relationships, but he should be careful. Hayes' mother said only that he should be ashamed of himself.

No adequate sex information was ever given Hayes by his parents. About the time his mother discovered the contraceptives he dropped in for a visit at the home of a neighbor where he stopped once in a while for a chat and to borrow reading material. On this occasion the woman who usually loaned him the books he wanted to read handed him a book on sexual adjustment in marriage, saying casually that she thought he might be interested in it. She had borrowed it from the local library. Sometime later a remark let slip by Hayes' mother established a connection, so that Hayes knew that she had secured the book herself, and had arranged to have it given to him by the neighbor.

The school gave Hayes no assistance in sex matters.

In fact the contrary was true. During one year he and some of his associates had a class with a young teacher whose manner of dress, habits of standing and sitting, and general behavior kept them constantly stimulated. This increased his preoccupation with sex and intensified his desires.

During his freshman year in college, Hayes read some authentic books on sex and had a number of discussions with a young physician who had just set up practice. Being of a very philosophic turn of mind and idealistic by nature, Hayes was attracted by the constructive emphasis on sex which came out of his talks with the doctor. About the same time he fell in love with a young woman whose high standards encouraged him to regard sex in a more idealistic fashion. The upshot was that after two years he had completely revised his point of view. Intercourse was dropped, and masturbation occurred two or three times a month.

During the summer that Hayes was twenty-two he worked with a road construction gang. Here again he met the old emphasis on sex and was much pleased to find that the discussions no longer held their former fascination. Instead he had a feeling of pity for those who placed sex on such a low level. To him it seemed that they were missing something very important and constructive.

The case studies in this chapter have been included to personalize the problems of sex adjustment. The individuals whose developmental histories you have just read are flesh and blood American youth. They have been educated in our public schools, and are being graduated from our colleges and universities. Their ex-

[203]

periences might well typify the experiences of many another youth. Since these experiences represent the personal histories of normal young men, they should serve to make the discussion of the preceding chapters more realistic—to help other young men to view their problems in a better perspective.

If this group of ten men could appear before you in person it would be your privilege to meet as clean-cut, as well-adjusted, as interested—and as interesting—a group of your contemporaries as one could reasonably expect to bring together. More successful than the average in their academic careers, in general satisfactorily adjusted in their social relationships, and wholesomely engrossed in the multifarious activities of the normal young man, they might be thought from outward appearances to have escaped the trials and perplexities of the average youth.

Yet with respect to sex behavior, their case histories show in varying degrees each of the forms of adjustment, together with the shifts and alterations, discussed in Chapter III. Their experiences in growing up emphasize the fact that sex is a chronological panorama, bringing new problems and new experiences from year to year—even from day to day. They demonstrate also the need for guidance and education in regard to sex during the entire period of growth and development. To answer the questions of a child at eight is not to provide him with adequate information for the problems of eighteen. Several were well informed concerning certain of the physical aspects, but most were wholly uninstructed with respect to the most helpful attitudes to assume or

[204]

the constructive side of sex. These young men have puzzled about, and experimented to find the most desirable forms of adjustment to follow. For the most part the usual misconceptions have been a part of their education. For some of them the problem of achieving an orderly self-control—of learning to live with sex—is still unsolved.

In growing up these young men have experienced some of life's tragedy—and some of its comedy as well. They have been the victims of ignorance and of sophistication; they have been the beneficiaries—though all too infrequently—of wise and helpful counsel. Several have had knowledge, but lacked wisdom; most of them have struggled against the fettering ties of ignorance. As a group one might say that the home, the church and the school have failed to give them the assistance to which they were entitled, and to the extent that they have achieved good adjustments, their own efforts must be commended.

To meet these young men, to talk with them personally, would bring to you the realization that meeting and solving problems is the common lot; and inspire the belief that worthy standards bring a genuine satisfaction in improved living. Out of the experience would grow an admiration for the courage and spirit with which these young men faced their problems and for the commendable qualities which they have displayed; there would come, too, an increased confidence in your own ability to cope with vital issues, and a determination to surmount the common obstacles which beset the path of anyone in the pursuit of better things.

[205]

GLOSSARY

Abortion, the process of giving birth to the embryo or fetus before it is able to sustain life. Often a miscarriage is produced or an operation performed to prevent the completion of the pregnancy.

Acne, an inflammatory skin disease of the sebaceous (oil) glands of the face and neck in particular. There is usually an eruption, often with pus formation. Usually found during adolescence.

Atypical, not typical.

Auto-erotic, pertaining to various forms of sex gratification induced by one's self alone. See Masturbation.

Coitus, sexual intercourse.

Conception, the union of the sperm cell and the egg which marks the beginning of pregnancy; the process of fertilization.

Contraception, the process of preventing, by various means, the occurrence of conception.

Ejaculation, in the male the expulsion of semen at the climax of intercourse, or in masturbation.

Embryo, the unborn child, from conception and through the first three months of pregnancy.

Erection, hardening and enlargement of the penis, the male sex organ.

Erogenous, pertaining to the sexually sensitive or sexually stimulating parts of the body.

Foetus, the unborn young; in man foetal life exists from the third month after conception until birth.

Genital organs, another term for the sexual organs, particularly the external organs.

Gonadal glands (gonads), sexual glands, ovary in the female, and testes in the male.

Gonorrhea, one of the venereal diseases, usually acquired through sexual intercourse.

Heterosexual, characterized by, or pertaining to, sexual interest in one of the other sex.

Homosexual, characterized by, or pertaining to, sexual interest in a member of one's own sex.

Masturbation, stimulation of one's own sexual organs to obtain sexual satisfaction; a phase of auto-eroticism.

Menstruation (menstrual period), a monthly discharge of blood or bloody fluid from the uterus of sexually mature females.

Miscarriage, the premature birth of the foetus.

Orgasm, the culmination or climax of sexual intercourse. Occurs in both sexes.

Ovulation, the elimination of the egg or ovum from the ovary.

Ovum, the female germ cell or egg. The fertilization of the ovum by the sperm cell of the male produces conception.

Penis, the male organ of coitus.

Pregnancy, the condition of carrying the unborn child from the period of conception to birth. The period of pregnancy in women is about nine months.

Puberty, the time at which a boy or girl becomes sexually capable of reproduction.

Pubic, pertaining to the pubis, the front portion of the pelvis. The pubic hair appears in the region surrounding the external reproductive organs.

Scrotum, the pouch below the penis which contains the testes or testicles.

Semen, the viscid, whitish fluid generated by the male reproductive organs. It contains the spermatozoa or sperm cells.

Seminal emission, the expulsion of semen at the time of orgasm. See Ejaculation.

Seminal vesicles, the small sacs which contain the semen.

Smegma, grayish-white substance produced by the sebaceous glands, which accumulates between the foreskin and the penis.

Spermatozoa (sperm cells), the male reproductive cells contained in the semen. A single ejaculation of semen contains innumerable spermatozoa.

Sublimation, diversion of energy from its original aim, specifically, redirection of sexual energy into some other activity, usually an activity of cultural or social worth.

Syphilis, the most serious of the venereal diseases, spread by infectious contacts, usually in sexual intercourse. A chancre or sore on the reproductive organs is the first symptom of infection.

Testes, testicles, the two male genital glands suspended in the scrotum; sometimes called the gonadal glands. These glands produce the sperm cells.

Urethra, the canal in the penis which carries off the urine in the male and serves also as the passage through which the semen leaves the body.

Uterus, the womb; a hollow organ in the female in which the unborn child develops.

Vagina, the canal which, in females, leads from the uterus to the external genital organs.

Vulva, the external parts of the female genital organs.

BIBLIOGRAPHY

BESIDES the books listed below persons interested in further reading in this field may secure pamphlets on various topics from the American Social Hygiene Association, 50 West 50th Street, New York City. The pamphlets cover such subjects as sex education, public health and medical problems of sex, legal and protective measures, family relationships, marriage adjustments, and the relationships of engaged couples.

Bromley, D. D. and Britten, F. H. *Youth and Sex.* New York: Harper and Brothers. 1938.
  A popularized discussion of the sexual behavior of over 1300 college men and women as determined by the use of questionnaires. Chiefly a description of current attitudes and practices. Offers little help in considering questions of adjustment.
Butterfield, Oliver M. *Marriage and Sexual Harmony.* New York: Emerson Books, Inc. 1937. 95 pp.
Butterfield, Oliver M. *Sex Life in Marriage.* New York: Emerson Books, Inc. 1938.
  The first title is a short, concise pamphlet largely confined to the sexual aspects of marriage. Clearly written but not technical. The second is a book covering the same topics.
Corner, George W. *Attaining Manhood.* New York: Harper and Brothers. 1938.
Corner, George W. *Attaining Womanhood.* New York: Harper and Brothers. 1939.

A clear and frank discussion, easily understood, of the anatomy and physiology of the reproductive system, and such other matters relating to an understanding of sex as might be of interest to boys and girls between the ages of 12 to 16. The first title is especially prepared for boys of this age and the second title for girls.

Dennett, Mary Ware. *Sex Education of Children.* New York: Vanguard Press. 1931.

A book for parents which elaborates on the need for objectivity in discussions of sex, and which will help in creating proper attitudes in relation to sex. A portion of the appendix is devoted to the diagrams and terms of sex anatomy and physiology.

Dennett, Mary Ware. *The Sex Side of Life.* New York, 350 West 55th Street: The author. 1919.

A brief but pointed description of desirable attitudes toward sex, the sexual relationships which should exist between boys and girls, men and women, and desirable forms of personal sex adjustments.

Dickerson, Roy E. *Growing into Manhood.* New York: Association Press. 1938.

A book for boys just entering the adolescent period.

Dickerson, Roy E. *So Youth May Know.* New York: Association Press. 1930.

One of the best books on male adjustments available for boys in the latter part of the adolescent period. Straight-forward, objective, and clear. Questions related to abstinence, promiscuity, petting, courtship, engagement and marriage are discussed. Includes anatomical description of both male and female sex organs.

Dunlap, Knight. *Civilized Life.* Baltimore: Williams and Wilkins. 1934.

Dunlap discusses the drives or urges which motivate

human behavior. Sex is presented here as one of eight other basic drives which influence human conduct.

Ellis, Havelock. *Little Essay of Love and Virtue*. New York City: Doubleday Doran. 1921.

Ellis, Havelock. *More Essays of Love and Virtue*. New York City: Doubleday Doran. 1931.

These two volumes contain a more or less philosophical discussion, simply presented, on such subjects as children and their duty to their parents, the meaning of purity and the play-function of sex, the objects of marriage and the marriage relationship. Prepared for youth.

Ellis, Havelock. *Psychology of Sex*. New York: Long and Smith. 1933.

Ellis, Havelock. *Studies in the Psychology of Sex*, Vols. I-IV. New York: Random House. 1936.

The last named reference to Havelock Ellis's works covers a four volume treatise which is probably too extensive and detailed except for those who want to make a comprehensive study of sexual problems. The first reference, a one volume work, is much more valuable to the average lay reader. It deals with sex as a normal human experience. Little discussion of abnormal manifestations. One of the most widely known books on the psychology of sex.

Everett, Millard S. *The Hygiene of Marriage*. New York: Vanguard Press. 1932.

A discussion of the psychological and physical aspects of marriage, including such topics as the physical and mental hygiene of sex and the need of a proper sex terminology, venereal diseases, and issues relating to contraception.

Exner, Max J. *The Question of Petting*. New York: Association Press. 1926.

Exner, Max J. *The Sexual Side of Marriage*. New York: W. W. Norton. 1932.

Two books which have been widely read. The discussions are presented in an able and lucid manner. "The Sexual Side of Marriage" stresses sex in relation to the total pattern of human behavior. Emphasizes other factors besides sex which enter into a successful marriage.

Folsom, J. K. *Plan For Marriage*. New York: Harper and Brothers. 1938.

A broad comprehensive approach to the marriage relationship. Questions relating to the earning and spending of money, parenthood and child rearing, companionship within marriage, emotional maturity, and the interplay of personalities are discussed. Provides excellent perspective for determining the place of sex in marriage.

Groves, E. R. and G. H. *Sex in Marriage*. New York: Macaulay Co. 1931.

Groves, E. R. and G. H. *Wholesome Marriage*. Boston: Houghton Mifflin Co. 1927.

These books are the result of the authors' long and comprehensive study of the various phases of marriage. They may be said to be "textbooks" in marriage.

Hamilton, G. V. and Macgowan, Kenneth. *What Is Wrong with Marriage?* New York City: Boni. 1929.

A research report of responses to questions relating to pre-marriage and marriage adjustments as given by both men and women.

Hart, Hornell N. and Ella B. *Personality and the Family*. New York: D. C. Heath and Company. 1935.

Included in this bibliography particularly for its comprehensive discussion of the effects of pre-marital and promiscuous sex relations. Also important in making clear that successful family living depends on adequate personality adjustments.

Mowrer, Ernest R. *The Family: Its Organization and Disorganization.* Chicago: University of Chicago Press. 1932.

A broad treatise on the general problems of the family, particularly with reference to problems of domestic organization and disorganization. Calls attention to the economic, recreational, and social functions of the family. This book induces a broader concept of the elements which go into successful marriage.

Mowrer, Harriet R. *Personality Adjustment and Domestic Discord.* New York: American Book Company. 1935.

A book for advanced students in problems of family adjustment. Emphasizes the personality aspects of family discord, the influence of social conditions on domestic adjustment, and methods of treatment. Included in bibliography because the work shows that sexual incompatibility may be only one cause of domestic disharmony, and that sexual difficulties may be the outgrowth of, or complicated by, other problems.

Parran, Thomas. *Shadow on the Land.* New York: Reynal and Hitchcock. 1937.

A comprehensive discussion of the venereal disease problem in the United States. A comparison is drawn with certain foreign countries, and suggestions are made for a campaign of eradication and prevention in this country.

Parshley, H. M. *The Science of Human Reproduction.* New York: Eugenics Publishing Co. 1933.

In this book sex is placed in broad perspective as a natural and normal function of both plant and animal life. It attempts "to answer most of the questions that non-professional students and intelligent laymen are likely to ask about the anatomy and physiology of human procreation."

Popenoe, Paul. *Modern Marriage.* New York City: Macmillan Company. 1935.

A book discussing the problems of marriage from a biological point of view. The sexual aspects of marriage are discussed, together with other features of the problems of mate selection and marriage.

Seabury, Florence G. *Love Is a Challenge.* New York: McGraw-Hill Book Co. 1936.

A stimulating discussion of the temperamental and psychological forces leading to marital happiness or discord.

Stone, Hannah and Abraham. *A Marriage Manual.* New York: Simon and Schuster. 1937.

A discussion in question-answer form of the sexual and reproductive aspects of marriage. Written in simple non-technical language, and very realistic in viewpoint. This book contains excellent references.

Terman, Louis M. *Psychological Factors in Marital Happiness.* New York: McGraw-Hill Book Company. 1938.

This report indicated that while successful marriage adjustments are influenced by sex other factors have a bearing also. A well-written and clearly presented report of a research on this topic.

Terman, Louis M. and Miles, Catherine Cox. *Sex and Personality.* New York City: McGraw-Hill Book Co. 1936.

A discussion of sex differences in personality and temperament, as determined through the use of a test to measure characteristics of masculinity and femininity. Three chapters are devoted to a discussion of homosexuality in males.

Wexberg, Erwin. *The Psychology of Sex.* New York City: Farrar & Rinehart. 1931.

[214]

A translation of the work of a German author, a follower of the Adlerian school of psychology. It is intended to serve as "an introduction to the psychology of sex for normal, intelligent adults."

Wile, Ira S. *The Sex Life of the Unmarried Adult*. New York: Vanguard Press. 1934.

An interpretation of current sex practices from the point of view of anthropology, biology, psychology, sociology, and similar approaches. For the more advanced student who is making a serious effort to understand the place of sex in our civilization.

Willoughby, Raymond R. *Sexuality in the Second Decade*. Washington, D. C.: Society for Research in Child Development. Vol. II, No. 3, Serial No. 10. 1937.

A summary of research in regard to such expressions of sexuality as auto-erotic practices and homosexual and heterosexual activities during adolescence.

Wright, Helena. *The Sex Factor in Marriage*. New York: Vanguard Press. 1937.

Presents the aesthetic interpretation of sex in marriage. The chief emphasis is upon sexual activities within marriage, and the nature and complexity of the sex relationship.

[215]